D0800825

The Adventures of Super3

The Adventures of Super3:

A Teacher's Guide to Information Literacy for Grades K-2

Annette C. H. Nelson and Danielle N. Dupuis

 LINWORTH

AN IMPRINT OF ABC-CLIO, LLC
Santa Barbara, California • Denver, Colorado • Oxford, England

Copyright 2010 by ABC-CLIO, LLC

All rights reserved. No part of this publication may be reproduced, stored in a retrieval system, or transmitted, in any form or by any means, electronic, mechanical, photocopying, recording, or otherwise, except for the inclusion of brief quotations in a review, without prior permission in writing from the publisher.

Library of Congress Cataloging-in-Publication Data
Nelson, Annette C. H.
   The adventures of Super3 : a teacher's guide to information literacy for grades K–2 / Annette C.H. Nelson and Danielle N. DuPuis.
      p. cm.
   Includes index.
   ISBN 978-1-58683-387-9 (acid-free paper) — ISBN 978-1-58683-413-5 (ebook)
1. Information literacy—Study and teaching (Primary)—United States.   2. Information literacy—Standards—United States.   I. DuPuis, Danielle N.   II. Title.
   ZA3075.N45   2010
   372.13—dc22   2010015460

ISBN: 978-1-58683-387-9
EISBN: 978-1-58683-413-5

14 13 12 11 10 1 2 3 4 5

This book is also available on the World Wide Web as an eBook.
Visit www.abc-clio.com for details.

Linworth
An Imprint of ABC-CLIO, LLC

ABC-CLIO, LLC
130 Cremona Drive, P.O. Box 1911
Santa Barbara, California 93116-1911

This book is printed on acid-free paper ∞

Manufactured in the United States of America

Contents

About the Authors

Photo courtesy of Fritzi Newton.

DANIELLE N. DUPUIS and ANNETTE C.H. NELSON became elementary school library media specialists in 2005 after graduating from the College of Information Studies at the University of Maryland. Prior to this Danielle worked as a public librarian for four years and Annette worked as an elementary classroom teacher for five years. The two enjoy teaming up to write creative lessons that not only educate, but also entertain their students. Danielle and Annette continue to work as elementary school library media specialists, making sure to demonstrate the importance of the field by making it an enjoyable learning experience for the school community.

Acknowledgments

We would like to thank Mike Eisenberg and Robert E. Berkowitz for creating the process of Super3 and allowing us to expand on their idea. We would also like to thank the hard workers at Plasq for making Comic Life our favorite application ever! On top of that they allowed us to use it when creating the worksheets for the lessons. Finally, we would like to thank Shaun Martin and Jay Gillen for taking our no-budget Super3 movie and making it amazing. We would like to dedicate this book to our everyday heroes: Danielle's Pop and Annette's brother, A.J.

DVD Contents

EPISODE 1: How Super3 Came to Be

EPISODE 2: Super3 and the Dinosaur Dilemma

SUPER3 MOVIE CREDITS

COMICS

GrKLess1Comic
GrKLess2Comic
GrKLess3Comic
Gr1Less1Comic
Gr1Less2Comic
Gr1Less3Comic
Gr2Less1Comic
Gr2Less2Comic
Gr3Less3Comic

POWERPOINT

Gr1Less3TextFeature

PRINTABLE MATERIALS

Super3StepCards
IntroLessEd
IntroLessReview
IntroLessKNotes
IntroLessKClues
IntroLessKClueFlip
IntroLessGr1Notes
IntroLessGr1&2ClueFlip
IntroLessGr2Notes
GrKLess1NewFriend
GrKLess1Pictures
GrKLess1Poster
GrKLess1Biography
GrKLess1Mod1NewFiriend
GrKLess1Mod2NewFriend
GrKLess2ColorCatastrophe
GrKLess2ColorChart
GrKLess2ColorCircles
GrKLess2Mod2ColorCatastrophe
GrKLess2Mod2Postcard
GrKLess3FirstAidFix
GrKLess3Pictures
GrKLess3Mod1FirstAidFix

GrKLess3Mod1Book
GrKLess3Mod1Captions
GrKLess3Mod2FirstAidFix
GrKLess3Mod2Book
Gr1Less1MysteriousWord
Gr1Less1VividVocab
Gr1Less1Dictionary
Gr1Less1Sort
Gr1Less1ModKMysteriousWord
Gr1Less1Mod2MysteriousWord
Gr1Less2PlanCards
Gr1Less2Petflyer
Gr1Less2Postcard
Gr1Less2Review
Gr1Less2ModKPostcard
Gr1Less2Mod2Postcard
Gr1Less3SnackAttack
Gr1Less3SuperSnacks
Gr1Less3Refrigerator
Gr1Less3Cabinet
Gr1Less3ModKSnackAttack
Gr1Less3ModKFavoriteSnack
Gr1Less3Mod2SnackAttack
Gr2Less1Lunch
Gr2Less1LostLunch
Gr2Less1PlanIdeas
Gr2Less1Maria'sSchedule
Gr2Less1ModKLostLunch
Gr2Less1Mod1LostLunch
Gr2Less2WeatherWorries
Gr2Less2WhatToWear
Gr2Less2ModKWeatherWorries
Gr2Less2ModKWhatToWear
Gr2Less2Mod1WeatherWorries
Gr2Less2Mod1WhatToWear
Gr2Less3InsectInvestigation
Gr2Less3LadybugLife
Gr2Less3PosterRubric
Gr2Less3Plan
Gr2Less3Review
Gr2Less3Diary
Gr2Less3ModK&1InsectInvestigation
Gr2Less3ModK&1PosterRubric
Gr2Less3ModKLadybugLife
Gr2Less3ModK&1Review
Gr2Less3Mod1LadybugLife

Standards and Permissions

The lessons in this book relate to several national education standards, including the American Association of School Librarians, Standards for the English Language Arts Sponsored by NCTE and IRA, and the National Committee on Science Education Standards and Assessment.

To assist in your planning we have included a selection of tables that list the lessons and the standards addressed by each.

American Association of School Librarians Standards for the 21st-Century Learner

All of the lessons included in this work correspond to many of the American Association of School Librarians Standards for the 21st-Century Learner. In the introductory lesson, "Super3 and the Dinosaur Dilemma," we demonstrate how to apply these standards. For more information about the AASL Standards for the 21st-Century Learner and to download a copy, please visit http://www.ala.org/aasl/standards.

National Science Education Standards, 1996

National Science Education Standards

Lesson	Standard
Kindergarten: Super3 and the First Aid Fix	**Science Content Standard F:** As a result of activities in grades K–4, all students should develop understanding of ✦ Personal health
Second Grade: Super3 and the Insect Investigation	**Life Science Content Standard C:** As a result of activities in grades K–4, all students should develop understanding of: ✦ Life cycles of organisms

Reprinted with permission from Barbara Murphy, Permissions Coordinator, 2009 by the National Academy of Sciences, Courtesy of the National Academies Press, Washington, D.C.

Standards for the English Language Arts Sponsored by NCTE and IRA

Lesson	Standard 3	Standard 5	Standard 7	Standard 8	Standard 12
Super3 and the Dinosaur Dilemma		x	x	x	
Kindergarten: Super3 and the New Friend			x		
Kindergarten: Super3 and the Color Catastrophe			x		
Kindergarten: Super3 and the First Aid Fix				x	

Standards for the English Language Arts Sponsored by NCTE and IRA (*Continued*)

Lesson	Standard 3	Standard 5	Standard 7	Standard 8	Standard 12
First Grade: Super3 and the Mysterious Word				x	
First Grade: Super3 and the Perfect Pet		x		x	x
First Grade: Super3 and the Snack Attack	x			x	
Second Grade: Super3 and the Lost Lunch				x	
Second Grade: Super3 and the Weather Worries				x	
Second Grade: Super3 and the Insect Investigation	x	x		x	

Standards for the English Language Arts, by the International Reading Association and the National Council of Teachers of English, Copyright 1996 by the International Reading Association and the National Council of Teachers of English. Reprinted with permission. A complete listing of the standards can be found at http://www.ncte.org/standards.

The Importance of Information Literacy

In today's society, information surrounds us like never before. Television, radio, print media, and the World Wide Web create access to billions of ideas and concepts. Learning how to sift through all that information for what is needed, or what concepts are important and valid, presents a challenge to many students. In an effort to help students with this overwhelming task, educators and librarians developed the concept of information literacy. "Students who are information literate are able to locate, interpret, organize and share information in a meaningful way" (ALA 2006). Educators need to design assignments to give students practice working with information and using higher-level thinking skills.

Though this need is great and recognized by many educators, it is not a simple task. Creating lessons that allow for guided practice of information literacy skills is often difficult when working with primary-aged children. The Super3 is an effective, simple method to help students understand what to do when they are faced with a project or problem. Encouraging a plan before beginning a project allows students time to slow down and think through the problem, and how it can be solved. Adding in a "review" step encourages students to think back and check over their work. The three steps of plan, do, and review make the problem less intimidating and possible to solve, even if you are five, six, or seven years old.

Super3's Transformation

In 2005, we began our journey as media specialists and knew information literacy was going to be an important concept in our media programs. However, we were unsure of how to accomplish this task. As a part of our county training, Bob Berkowitz conducted a professional development session and introduced us to the Super3 and Big6. We both enjoyed the presentation and left the session feeling excited and eager to collaborate on lesson plan ideas. Being a product of *Sesame Street*, Annette came up with the idea that students would find the process of Super3 easier to comprehend if it was actually a superhero number three. The idea that you would use the steps of plan, do, and review (the Super3) to help you solve your problem would be easy for young students to understand. Danielle sketched out an idea for a puppet character, and together we went shopping for materials. Later that week, Super3 was born out of foam, fabric, some red spray paint, and a lot of love!

Being fans of multimedia, we decided to make a video to introduce Super3 and show how he transformed from an ordinary number three into Super3. We came up with a script for Super3's creation, and soon we were making our own Super3 creation movie to share with our classes. When we each taught the process of the Super3 using our superhero character for the first time, we were amazed by the kindergarteners' reactions. In simply showing students the puppet character we created, and without telling the students his name, they all cried out "Super3!" Through their prior knowledge of superheroes and comics, they instinctively knew that this number three with a blue cape was a superhero. After showing the movie, we both would begin subsequent Super3 lessons by singing out "Dun Dun Da Da!" and the students automatically responded with gleeful cries of "Super3!" Every time the students faced an information problem, or any kind of problem, and did not remember what process to use, we reminded them by singing out "Dun Dun Da Da!"

How to Use this Book

To begin using this book, start with the video short, "Episode One: How Super3 Came to Be," which explains the transformation of "Little3" into "Super3." Once the students are introduced to the character, all grade levels (K–2) can participate in the introductory lesson of "Super3 and the Dinosaur Dilemma." Here Super3 goes on his first adventure, shown in a video, and helps a student named Kayla with a dinosaur project. After watching the video, students help another child, Eddie, complete the same project with a different dinosaur. Once you have taught the introductory lesson, you are ready to move on to the grade-level-specific lessons. This book includes three lessons, complete with worksheets, for each grade level; kindergarten, first, and second. Each lesson includes modified worksheets and instructions so they can be used with any grade K–2. If you are a teacher-librarian, you may only wish to teach the three lessons specific to each grade. However, a classroom teacher may use the modifications to teach all nine lessons to his or her students. The lessons are based around national standards for media and language arts and other pertinent curriculum areas in order to address objectives covered in the classroom.

All of the lessons begin with a quick engagement comic to grab the students' attention. Each of the nine comics introduces the problem of the lesson faced by Super3 and a student. Students work as a group to create and carry out a plan. Teachers or teacher-librarians bring closure to the lesson by reviewing the plan and product, and reviewing how the Super3 helped the students solve the problem. If there is extra time, a list of suggested books that correlate with the subject of the lesson provide extension opportunities. Worksheets or opportunities for anecdotal evidence provide assessment methods for the teacher or teacher-librarian. All the materials needed are listed in the lesson, and the necessary worksheets for each lesson are provided. The labeling system for each provided worksheet or material is as follows:

Grade Level	Lesson Sequence	Modification Level (if necessary)	Name of worksheet (often abbreviated)

Gr2Less3Mod1LadybugLife is the modified second-grade worksheet designed for use with first graders, entitled "A Ladybug's Life." If there is no modification level included in the worksheet label, then it is for the grade level for which it was originally intended.

Promoting Super3

Once you have established the use of Super3 in your program, you may want to spread the word to the rest of the staff in your building. One of the benefits of the Super3 learning strategy is that it can be used across all curricular areas. You could conduct a professional development session, showing staff how to incorporate the Super3 steps of plan, do, and review into their everyday instruction. If you'd like, show the Super3 video, "Episode One: How Super3 Came to Be." You may also wish to make copies of the Super3 Step Cards to distribute to other educators in your building to use with students. When students realize that Super3 isn't a concept used in just one class, they will be more likely to apply it when encountering a project or problem. For more resources on how to incorporate the Super3 with your staff or students, visit http://www.big6.com.

We believe that when students enjoy the learning process, they retain more information and gain a deeper understanding of the concept. We hope you find the lessons easy to understand and implement. These lessons are designed to be richly educational for the students and very entertaining. Hopefully this book will enable you to create more of your own Super3 lessons and help your students remember that if they ever face a problem all they have to do is call on the Super3!

—Danielle and Annette

Reference

American Library Association. "Information Literacy: Unlocking Your Child's Door to the World" (2006), http://www.ala.org/ala/aasl/schlibrariesandyou/parentsandcomm/informationliteracy.htm.

CHAPTER 1

Introductory Lesson

Super3 and the Dinosaur Dilemma

Kindergarten, First Grade, or Second Grade

AASL Standards for the 21st-Century Learner

Standard 1: Inquire, think critically, and gain knowledge.

Standard 2: Draw conclusions, make informed decisions, apply knowledge to new situations, and create new knowledge.

Specific standard strands are embedded throughout the lesson.

Excerpted from Standards for the 21st-Century Learner, *by the American Association of School Librarians, a division of the American Library Association, copyright © 2007 American Library Association. Available for download at http://www.ala.org/aasl/standards. Used with permission.*

Performance Objectives

✦ Students will state the three steps of the Super3.

✦ Students will describe the problem faced by Eddie.

✦ Students will research information about a Tyrannosaurus Rex.

- ✦ Students will compose clues about a Tyrannosaurus Rex and create a clue flipper.
- ✦ Students will judge their work to determine how well their completed product solved the problem.

Lesson Timeframe

Two 40-minute lessons

Provided Materials

For Teaching All Grade Levels

- ✦ Copy of "Super3 Step Cards" (Super3StepCards)
- ✦ Copy of "Dinosaur Assignment" (IntroLessEd)
- ✦ Copy of "Eddie's Review" (IntroLessReview)
- ✦ DVD of "Super3 and the Dinosaur Dilemma"

For Teaching Kindergarten

- ✦ Copies for each student of "Dinosaur Dilemma" (IntroLessKNotes)
- ✦ Copies for each student of "Dinosaur Clues" (IntroLessKClues)
- ✦ Copies for each student of "What Dinosaur Am I?" (IntroLessKClueFlip)

For Teaching First Grade

- ✦ Copies for each student of "Dinosaur Dilemma" (IntroLessGr1Notes)
- ✦ Copies for each student of "What Dinosaur Am I?" (IntroLessGr1&2ClueFlip)

For Teaching Second Grade

- ✦ Copies for each student of "Dinosaur Dilemma" (IntroLessGr2Notes)
- ✦ Copies for each student of "What Dinosaur Am I?" (IntroLessGr1&2ClueFlip)

Materials You Will Need

- ✦ TV/DVD player or computer/LCD projector
- ✦ Soft ball or beach ball
- ✦ Pencils

Preparation Before Lesson

- ✦ Read over the lesson and determine which idea for the plan you would like the students to use to solve the problem.
- ✦ Gather the materials needed to complete your selected plan (e.g., newspapers, telephone with speakerphone, or computers with Internet access).

Engagement

Day One

1. Display the movie "Super3 and the Dinosaur Dilemma" to the students.
2. Ask students to name the steps of the Super3.

Activity

3. Explain to the students that they need to help another student in Kayla's class named Eddie.
4. Display either an electronic copy or color transparency of "Dinosaur Assignment" (IntroLessEd).
5. Ask students to describe Eddie's assignment (He is supposed to write clues about a Tyrannosaurus Rex).
6. Prompt students to come up with a source in which to find clues about a Tyrannosaurus Rex. Suggestions include:

   a. In a book

   b. In an encyclopedia (print or electronic)

   c. On Web pages, such as "Tyrannosaurus Rex" on the site *Enchanted Learning* (2009), http://www.enchantedlearning.com/subjects/dinosaurs/dinos/Trex.shtml.

7. Once you have determined the plan as a class, explain that when taking notes, you only write down the key words of the sentence so as to avoid plagiarism. Explain plagiarism to students as stealing someone else's ideas and using them as their own idea.

The next step demonstrates the AASL Standards for the 21st-Centry Learner Strand:

Responsibilities 1.3.3: Follow ethical and legal guidelines in gathering and using information.

8. Instruct students to record the source of their information at the top of their page.

The next step demonstrates the AASL Standards for the 21st-Centry Learner Strand:

Skills 1.1.6: Read, view, and listen for information presented in any format (e.g., textual, visual, media, digital) in order to make inferences and gather meaning.

9. Choose one of the following strategies for research depending on the level of your students:

   a. Kindergarten: Using your source, complete the "Dinosaur Dilemma" worksheet (IntroLessKNotes). This should be done as a whole group. Display a copy of the note-taking sheet and, as you read information from your source, fill in the blanks together as a class. Circulate around the class to assist them in following along.

   b. First Grade: Using the source of your choice, complete the "Dinosaur Dilemma" worksheet (IntroLessGr1Notes). Display a copy of the note-taking sheet and, as you read information from your source, fill in the information together as a class.

Complete the first two as a whole group, but then have students work with a partner to find the other two facts.

    c. Second Grade: Model how to take notes from the source on the Tyrannosaurs Rex for the class by reading aloud the first few sentences and writing down three or four words about a fact you feel is important. Then, allow students to complete the rest of the facts by using their own copy of the source. They can complete the "Dinosaur Dilemma" worksheet (IntroLessGr2Notes) independently or with a partner. Circulate among the students to keep them on task and assist when needed.

10. Close the day's lesson by reviewing the steps of the Super3 and discussing what the students have left to complete: write the clues to make the flip book and review.

Day Two

11. Remind students they are helping Eddie complete his dinosaur flip book for school. The students completed research about the Tyrannosaurus Rex in the previous class and now need to write their clues.

12. Distribute the "Dinosaur Dilemma" worksheet students used in the previous lesson to record their notes.

The next step demonstrates the AASL Standards for the 21st-Centry Learner Strand:

Skills 2.1.2 Organize knowledge so that it is useful.

13. Demonstrate how to turn the notes into clues about the Tyrannosaurus Rex. Read a note taken and then ask students for sample sentences they could write. To complete the book follow one of the suggestions below, depending on your students' ability level:

    a. Kindergarten: Distribute "Dinosaur Clues" (IntroLessKClues) and read each one aloud to the class. Ask students to cross out the ones that are not clues about the Tyrannosaurus Rex. Have students cut and paste the clues into the boxes on the "What Dinosaur Am I?" sheet (IntroLessKClueFlip). Show students how to cut out the boxes on the top sheet so you can lift them up and see what is underneath. Then have students paste the top sheet on top of the clues so they are hidden but can be seen when the flaps are lifted.

    b. First Grade: Distribute the "What Dinosaur Am I?" sheet (IntroLessGr1&2ClueFlip) and demonstrate how to write the first two clues. Allow students time to work independently or with a partner to write the last two clues. Show students how to cut out the boxes on the top sheet so you can lift them up and see what is underneath. Students should then paste the top sheet on top of the clues so they are hidden but can be seen when the flaps are lifted.

    c. Second Grade: Distribute the "What Dinosaur Am I?" sheet (IntroLessGr1&2ClueFlip) and demonstrate how to write the first clue. Allow students to work independently or with a partner to write the last clues. Show students how to cut out the boxes on the top sheet so you can lift them up and see what is underneath. Have students paste the top sheet on top of the clues so they are hidden but can be seen when the flaps are lifted.

The next step demonstrates the AASL Standards for the 21st-Centry Learner Strand:

Dispositions in Action 2.2.4: Demonstrate personal productivity by completing products to express learning.

14. As students complete the flip book, circulate and assist where needed.

15. You can have students share their clues with others at their table or just move on to the Review step.

The next step demonstrates the AASL Standards for the 21st-Centry Learner Strands:

Self-Assessment Strategies 3.4.1: Assess the process by which learning was achieved in order to revise strategies and learn more effectively in the future.

Self-Assessment Strategies 3.4.2: Assess the quality and effectiveness of the learning product.

16. Display an electronic or transparency copy of "Eddie's Review" (IntroLessReview) for the students. As you ask each question, toss a soft ball to each student raising his or her hand to speak. Once the student has finished, have them toss it back to you.

Closure

17. Ask students to recall the three steps of the Super3 and explain how they used the steps to solve the Dinosaur Dilemma.

Assessment

18. Collect and grade the "Dinosaur Dilemma" worksheet (IntroLessKNotes / IntroLessGr1Notes / IntroLessGr2Notes)

19. Collect and grade "What Dinosaur Am I?" (IntroLessKClueFlip/ IntroLessGr1&2ClueFlip)

Suggested Books

Aliki. *My Visit to the Dinosaurs.* New York: Crowell, 1985.

Andreae, Giles. *Captain Flinn and the Pirate Dinosaurs.* New York: Margaret K. McElderry Books, 2005.

Broach, Elise. *When Dinosaurs Came with Everything.* New York: Atheneum Books for Young Readers, 2007.

Most, Bernard. *How Big Were the Dinosaurs.* Orlando, FL: Red Wagon Books, 2008.

Willems, Mo. *Edwina, the Dinosaur Who Didn't Know She Was Extinct.* New York: Hyperion Books for Children, 2006.

Yolen, Jane. *How Do Dinosaurs Go to School?* New York: Blue Sky Press, 2007.

Directions: Use these Super3 step cards with your class. These smaller step cards are perfect for a pocket chart. There are also larger step cards attached if you prefer to make a mini-poster of the step cards for display in your classroom/ library media center.

Plan

Do

Review

plan

Do

Review

Dinosaur Assignment

Dear Students,

   You learned about dinosaurs in science class. I will assign each of you a specific dinosaur to learn more about. Use a resource to find out some facts about your dinosaur. Once you have recorded several facts, you should complete a guessing game flip book to share with the class.

Sincerely,

Ms. Wright

Eddie—
Your assignment
is the Tyrannosaurus
Rex.

From *The Adventures of Super3: A Teacher's Guide to Information Literacy for Grades K–2* by Annette C. H. Nelson and Danielle N. DuPuis. Santa Barbara, CA: Linworth. Copyright © 2010.

Review your Dinosaur Flip Book:

1. Did you locate facts about the Tyrannosaurus Rex? _____

2. Did you record where you found your information? _____

3. Did you create your flip book and include all the clues you needed? _____

4. Did you put your name on all your papers? _____

5. Are you proud of your work? _____

Review Your Process:

1. What did you do well this time? _____

_____

2. Where did you find your information? _____

_____

3. Was it a good place to look? _____

From *The Adventures of Super3: A Teacher's Guide to Information Literacy for Grades K–2* by Annette C. H. Nelson and Danielle N. DuPuis. Santa Barbara, CA: Linworth. Copyright © 2010.

Name: _____Kindergarten

Dinosaur Dilemma

Problem: Eddie needs to make a Tyrannosaurus Rex guessing game.

Plan

I will take notes about the Tyrannosaurus Rex for my guessing game from a(n)

Circle the source you will use.

Encyclopedia   Web site   Book

Notes about the Tyrannosaurus Rex

1. _____ feet long

2. Lived _____

years ago

3. Walked on _____ legs

4. It was a _____,

meaning it ate meat

From *The Adventures of Super3: A Teacher's Guide to Information Literacy for Grades K–2* by Annette C. H. Nelson and Danielle N. DuPuis. Santa Barbara, CA: Linworth. Copyright © 2010.

Dinosaur Clues

Directions: Cross out the clues that do not belong. Cut out the correct clues to paste into your Dinosaur Flip Book.

I ate plants	I ate meat

I walked on 2 legs

I walked on 4 legs

I am still alive	I am extinct

I was 6 feet long

I was 40 feet long

From *The Adventures of Super3: A Teacher's Guide to Information Literacy for Grades K–2* by Annette C. H. Nelson and Danielle N. DuPuis. Santa Barbara, CA: Linworth. Copyright © 2010.

What Dinosaur Am I?

Clue # 1

Clue # 2

Clue # 3

Answer

From *The Adventures of Super3: A Teacher's Guide to Information Literacy for Grades K–2* by Annette C. H. Nelson and Danielle N. DuPuis. Santa Barbara, CA: Linworth. Copyright © 2010.

Directions:
1. Glue 3 out of your 4 clues in each of the boxes below.
2. Cut ONLY on the dotted lines of the page titled, "Which Dinosaur Am I?"
3. Place glue on the areas of this sheet marked, "GLUE."
4. Gently place the first sheet on top of this one.

GLUE

GLUE

GLUE

Glue your 1st clue here

GLUE

GLUE   GLUE

GLUE

Glue your 2nd clue here

GLUE

GLUE   GLUE

GLUE

Glue your 3rd clue here

GLUE

GLUE   GLUE   GLUE

GLUE

Tyrannosaurus Rex!

GLUE   GLUE

From *The Adventures of Super3: A Teacher's Guide to Information Literacy for Grades K–2* by Annette C. H. Nelson and Danielle N. DuPuis. Santa Barbara, CA: Linworth. Copyright © 2010.

Name: _____1st grade

Dinosaur Dilemma

Problem: Eddie needs to make a Tyrannosaurus Rex guessing game.

Plan

I will take notes about the Tyrannosaurus Rex for my guessing game from

_____

Write the book or Web site name here.

Notes about the Tyrannosaurus Rex

1. _____ feet tall

2. Lived _____ years ago

3. Its name means _____ _____

4. It was a _____, meaning it ate meat

From *The Adventures of Super3: A Teacher's Guide to Information Literacy for Grades K–2* by Annette C. H. Nelson and Danielle N. DuPuis. Santa Barbara, CA: Linworth. Copyright © 2010.

What Dinosaur Am I?

Clue # 1

Clue # 2

Clue # 3

Answer

From *The Adventures of Super3: A Teacher's Guide to Information Literacy for Grades K–2* by Annette C. H. Nelson and Danielle N. DuPuis. Santa Barbara, CA: Linworth. Copyright © 2010.

GLUE

GLUE

Directions:
1. Write each of your 3 clues and the answer in the lined boxes below.
2. Cut ONLY on the dotted lines of the page titled, "Which Dinosaur Am I?"
3. Place glue on the areas of this sheet marked, "GLUE."
4. Gently place the first sheet on top of this one.

GLUE

GLUE

GLUE

GLUE   GLUE

GLUE

GLUE

GLUE   GLUE

GLUE

GLUE

GLUE   GLUE   GLUE

GLUE

GLUE   GLUE

From *The Adventures of Super3: A Teacher's Guide to Information Literacy for Grades K–2* by Annette C. H. Nelson and Danielle N. DuPuis. Santa Barbara, CA: Linworth. Copyright © 2010.

Name: _____2nd Grade

Dinosaur Dilemma

Problem: Eddie needs to make a Tyrannosaurus Rex guessing game.

Plan

I will take notes about the Tyrannosaurus Rex for my guessing game from

_____

Write the book or Web site name here.

Notes about the Tyrannosaurus Rex

1. _____

2. _____

3. _____

_____

4. _____

_____

5. _____

_____

From *The Adventures of Super3: A Teacher's Guide to Information Literacy for Grades K–2* by Annette C. H. Nelson and Danielle N. DuPuis. Santa Barbara, CA: Linworth. Copyright © 2010.

CHAPTER 2

Teaching Super3 to Kindergarten

Teachers and teacher-librarians who work with kindergarteners know the importance of structured, engaging lessons that break down difficult concepts into accessible pieces. The Super3 process is easy for these young students to implement once they understand the intent of the steps.

By introducing the concept of Super3 as a superhero, even kindergarteners are able to remember the names of the steps. With practice, students will be able to use the Super3 when they encounter a problem. You will find it rewarding to teach a lesson that provides the students with meaningful, exciting activities, and then to see the students subsequently *remember* the concepts you taught them.

This chapter includes three lessons developed specifically for kindergarten students. The lessons begin with problems younger students can easily relate to, and they gradually become more academic in terms of research. In "Super3 and the New Friend," students design a poster to advertise Joel to the other students in his class. This will help him make a friend at his new school. Lesson 2, "Super3 and the Color Catastrophe," has kindergarteners combining colors to make new colors, in order to help Madison finish her art project. Various ways to find the information are provided so you can choose the method that works best for your class. In the final lesson, "Super3 and the First-Aid Fix," Super3 helps Desiree remember how to take care of cuts. Here students research basic first aid and sequentially order pictures of each step to create a visual aid. Each of the three lessons includes a modified activity for use with first or second grade. If your kindergarten class is particularly capable, you might want to use one of these activities. Enjoy the adventures that follow!

Lesson 1: Super3 and the New Friend
Performance Objectives

- ✦ Students will name the steps of the Super3.
- ✦ Students will design a plan to solve the problem presented.
- ✦ Student will create a poster to advertise for a friend.

Lesson Timeframe

30 minutes

Provided Materials

- ✦ Copy of "Super3 and the New Friend" comic (GrKLess1Comic)—Display either a color transparency or electronic PDF version
- ✦ Copy of "Super3 Step Cards" (Super3StepCards)
- ✦ Copies for each student of "The New Friend" (GrKLess1NewFriend)
- ✦ Copies of "Friend Pictures" (GrKLess1Pictures)
- ✦ Copies of "Friend Poster" (GrKLess1Poster) (this should be copied onto the other side of "The New Friend" [GrKLess1NewFriend])
- ✦ "Joel's Biography" (GrKLess1Biography)

Materials You Will Need

- ✦ Overhead projector or LCD projector and computer
- ✦ Optional: Document camera
- ✦ Pencils
- ✦ Soft ball to toss

Engagement

1. Have students stand in a circle. Explain to students that they need to think of a word to describe a good friend. Students will pass their ball on to a friend in the circle and clearly say the word they think describes a good friend. The person that receives the ball will pass it to another student in the circle as they state their word. Play will continue until all the students in the class have had a turn.

Activity

2. Display the copy of "Super3 and the New Friend" comic (GrKLess1Comic).

3. Read the comic aloud and ask students what process Super3 should use to help him solve his problem (answer: the Super3).

4. Have students recall the steps of the Super3 and display each step as they name it using the "Super3 Step Cards" (Super3StepCards).

5. Instruct students to brainstorm ways that Joel could find a new friend. Select several students to share their answers with the class. Then ask students to look again at the "Super3 and the New Friend" comic. Ask students if they can see any picture clues in the comic that might give them an idea on how they could help Joel find a new friend. (Be sure and point out the billboard advertisement if students can't find it by themselves.)

6. After students volunteer their answers, explain that they will be creating a poster to advertise for a friend for Joel.

7. Distribute the "The New Friend" (GrKLess1NewFriend) worksheet.

8. Read over the plan section and ask students to check all of the boxes that describe a part of their plan.

9. Explain that in order to create a poster to advertise for a friend for Joel, they must learn about Joel and figure out what he likes.

10. Read "Joel's Biography" (GrKLess1Biography) aloud to the students.

11. After reading the biography, ask students what qualities or things Joel might look for when searching for a friend. Ask students to cite examples from the text. As students give their answers, write them on the board so that everyone can see the answers.

12. Next, distribute the "Friend Pictures" (GrKLess1Pictures) to students and explain that they need to find only the pictures that describe Joel. They should then cut out the pictures and glue them around the image of Joel on the "Friend Poster" (GrKLess1Poster) to create an advertisement to help find a friend for Joel.

13. Students may color their posters to complete their work.

Closure

14. Read the review questions and ask that students follow along and circle the appropriate answers.

Assessment

15. Collect and grade "The New Friend" (GrKLess1NewFriend).

Modifications

For Use with First Grade

+ Use first grade modified version of "The New Friend" (GrKLess1Mod1NewFriend).

+ Omit the use of "Friend Pictures" (GrKLess1Pictures), and have students create their own pictures and words for the poster. Together as a class, brainstorm a list of words that the students can use. Write these on the board or on a place where the students can see them.

For Use with Second Grade

✦ Use second grade modified version of "The New Friend" (GrKLess1Mod2NewFriend).

✦ Omit the use of "Friend Pictures" (GrKLess1Pictures), and have students create their own pictures and words for the poster.

Suggested Books

Carlson, Nancy. *How to Lose All Your Friends.* New York: Viking, 1994.

Keller, Holly. *Help!: A Story of Friendship.* New York: Greenwillow Books, 2007.

Lionni, Leo. *Little Blue and Little Yellow.* 1959. New York: Mulberry Books, 1994.

Rohmann, Eric. *My Friend Rabbit.* Brookfield, CT: Roaring Brook Press, 2002.

Watt, Melanie. *Scaredy Squirrel Makes a Friend.* New York: Kids Can Press, 2007.

Willems, Mo. *Leonardo the Terrible Monster.* New York: Hyperion Books for Children, 2005.

Name: _____Kindergarten

The New Friend

Problem: Joel doesn't know how to make a friend.

Plan

Check off the boxes to show your plan.

☐ Make a poster about Joel.   ☐ Walk a dog.

☐ Bake a cake.   ☐ Do your homework.

☐ Learn about Joel.   ☐ Collect crayons and pictures

Do

Okay, now create your poster. Cut out pictures that describe Joel and place them around Joel's picture. When you are finished, color your poster to complete your job!

Review

Circle Yes or No to answer each question.

Did I use pictures in an interesting way?

Yes   No

Is there anything I need to do before I turn in my poster?   Yes   No

From *The Adventures of Super3: A Teacher's Guide to Information Literacy for Grades K–2* by Annette C. H. Nelson and Danielle N. DuPuis. Santa Barbara, CA: Linworth. Copyright © 2010.

From *The Adventures of Super3: A Teacher's Guide to Information Literacy for Grades K–2* by Annette C. H. Nelson and Danielle N. DuPuis. Santa Barbara, CA: Linworth. Copyright © 2010.

From *The Adventures of Super3: A Teacher's Guide to Information Literacy for Grades K–2* by Annette C. H. Nelson and Danielle N. DuPuis. Santa Barbara, CA: Linworth. Copyright © 2010.

Joel's Biography

Before moving, Joel played soccer with his friends every afternoon. Since he moved, he has been playing jump rope with his younger sister, but he doesn't like it very much. He helps his mother around the house by taking out the trash and feeding his favorite pet dog, Sparky. Joel looks forward to Friday because his dad brings home pizza! He doesn't like Mondays because his mom serves spaghetti-- a food he doesn't enjoy at all! Joel is hoping to meet a friend who likes the same things that he likes. Will you be his friend?

From *The Adventures of Super3: A Teacher's Guide to Information Literacy for Grades K–2* by Annette C. H. Nelson and Danielle N. DuPuis. Santa Barbara, CA: Linworth. Copyright © 2010.

Name: _____1st Grade

The New Friend

Problem: Joel doesn't know how to make a friend.

Plan

Check off the boxes to show your plan.

☐ Make a poster about Joel.   ☐ Walk a dog.

☐ Bake a cake.   ☐ Do your homework.

☐ Learn about Joel.   ☐ List words that describe Joel.

Do

Okay, now create your poster. Draw pictures that describe what Joel likes. Then, write 3 adjectives that describe a good friend to place around Joel's picture. When you are finished, color your poster to complete your job!

Review

Circle Yes or No to answer each question.

Did I do everything I was supposed to do?

Yes   No

Is there anything I need to do before I turn in my poster?   Yes   No

---

From *The Adventures of Super3: A Teacher's Guide to Information Literacy for Grades K–2* by Annette C. H. Nelson and Danielle N. DuPuis. Santa Barbara, CA: Linworth. Copyright © 2010.

Name: _____2nd Grade

The New Friend

Problem: Joel doesn't know how to make a friend.

Plan
Write your plan in the space provided.

I will _____

_____

Do
Okay, now create your poster. Around Joel, write words and draw pictures that describe Joel. When you are finished, color your poster to complete your job!

Review
Did I do everything I was supposed to do?

Yes   No

Is there anything I need to do before I turn in my poster?   Yes   No

Do I think my poster will help Joel find a friend?

Yes   No

Circle Yes or No to answer each question.

From *The Adventures of Super3: A Teacher's Guide to Information Literacy for Grades K–2* by Annette C. H. Nelson and Danielle N. DuPuis. Santa Barbara, CA: Linworth. Copyright © 2010.

Lesson 2: Super3 and the Color Catastrophe
Performance Objectives

✦ Students will recall the steps of the Super3.

✦ Students will create a poster by mixing primary colors.

✦ Students will review their product and process to determine if they were successful.

Lesson Timeframe

35 minutes

Provided Materials

✦ Copy of "Super3 and the Color Catastrophe" comic (GrKLess2Comic)—Display either a color transparency or electronic PDF version

✦ Copy of "Super3 Step Cards" (Super3StepCards)

✦ Copies for each student of "Color Catastrophe" (GrKLess2ColorCatastrophe)

✦ Copies for each student of "Madison's Color Chart" (GrKLess2ColorChart)—may be copied on the back of the "Color Catastrophe"

✦ Color transparency of "Color Circles" (GrKLess2ColorCircles)

Materials You Will Need

✦ Overhead projector or LCD projector and computer

✦ Optional: Document camera

✦ Pencils and crayons

✦ Optional: Artist costume

Choose one set of materials below:

✦ Pastel chalks in red, blue, and yellow

✦ Watercolor paints / water / small cups / cotton swabs or paint brushes

✦ Poster paints / water / small cups / cotton swabs or paint brushes

✦ Color transparency of "Color Circles" (GrKLess2ColorCircles)

Engagement

1. Optional: Greet students dressed as an artist.

2. Display the copy of "Super3 and the Color Catastrophe" comic (GrKLess2Comic) for the

students. Read the comic aloud and ask students what process Super3 should use to help him solve his problem (answer: the Super3).

3. Have students recall the steps of the Super3 and display each step as they name it using the "Super3 Step Cards" (Super3StepCards).

Activity

4. Remind students that when making a plan you should list all the possible solutions to the problem before selecting the best one.

5. Ask students to think of ways they could help Madison get more colors for her painting. List students' ideas on the board. More than likely, the students will suggest mixing the colors.

6. Explain that students should make something to help Madison remember what colors mix together to create others. Guide students to suggest making a color chart Madison can hang up.

7. Distribute copies of "Color Catastrophe" (GrKLess2ColorCatastrophe) to each student.

8. Look over each suggestion and discuss the positives and negatives of each idea. As a group, choose the plan that would work best for your class.

   a. Suggested: Use a document camera or a large piece of paper on the board to show how to mix colors using pastel chalk. You can quickly mark each student's copy of "Madison's Color Chart" (GrKLess2ColorChart) with the two colors and let them mix them with their fingers. Repeat the procedure until all three "new" colors are made.

   b. You may also decide to "mix" the colors using an overhead projector and "Color Circles" (GrKLess2ColorCircles). Students could use crayons to record what colors resulted from mixing blue, yellow, and red on "Madison's Color Chart" (GrKLess2ColorChart).

   c. You might instead choose to demonstrate mixing paint (poster or watercolors) in front of the students. Students could use crayons to record what colors resulted from mixing blue, yellow, and red on "Madison's Color Chart" (GrKLess2ColorChart).

   d. The final option is that the students actually use paint to mix their own colors on "Madison's Color Chart" (GrKLess2ColorChart).

9. Once the students have discovered how to help Madison find more colors for her painting, allow time to review their work. Read the "Review" section of the "Color Catastrophe" (GrKLess2ColorCatastrophe) worksheet with the students and instruct students to check off the boxes that reflect their feelings.

Closure

10. Ask students to recall what process they used to help Madison solve her problem (the Super3).

11. Ask students to recall what new colors each of the color combinations could make (red + yellow = orange / red + blue = purple / blue + yellow = green).

Assessment

12. Collect and grade "Color Catastrophe" (GrKLess2ColorCatastrophe) and "Madison's Color Chart" (GrKLess2ColorChart).

Modifications

For Use with First Grade

✦ Complete the lesson as suggested for kindergarten. However, you could also introduce the concept of primary (red, blue, yellow) and secondary (green, orange, purple) colors by looking up more information on a Web site about mixing colors. You can also ask the art teacher to visit for a minilesson.

For Use with Second Grade

✦ Use the modified second grade worksheet, "Color Catastrophe" (GrKLess2Mod2Color-Catastrophe). Instead of students simply mixing the paint colors to determine what new colors are made, have students write Madison a postcard to explain what she can do with her blue, red, and yellow paints. Copy and distribute the worksheet, "Madison's Postcard" (GrKLess2Mod2Postcard), to each student. On the front of the postcard show them how to color the circles so that each shows two primary colors (red, blue, yellow) making a secondary color (green, orange, purple). Then instruct students to write a note to Madison explaining how she can mix the colors herself.

Suggested Books

Beaumont, Karen. *I Ain't Gonna Paint No More!* Orlando, FL: Harcourt, 2005.

Carle, Eric. *Hello, Red Fox.* New York: Simon & Schuster, 1998.

Fontes, Justine. *Black Meets White.* Cambridge, MA: Candlewick Press, 2005.

Martin, Bill. *Brown Bear, Brown Bear, What Do You See?* 1967. New York: Henry Holt, 1992.

Seuss, Dr. *My Many Colored Days.* New York: Knopf, 1996.

Walsh, Ellen Stoll. *Mouse Paint.* Orlando, FL: Harcourt, 1995.

Name: _____

Color Catastrophe

Problem: Madison needs to remember what colors to mix together.

Plan
Check off the box that shows your plan.

- ☐ Write Madison a letter
- ☐ Tie a string around Madison's finger
- ☐ Look in a book.
- ☐ Create a color chart poster so she remembers mixing

Do
Do your plan on the back of this paper.

Review
Circle or write your answer to the questions.

Did I help Madison find the colors she needed and remember how they mix together?   Yes   No

When can you use this again?
- ☐ in art class
- ☐ when I make a snack
- ☐ at home when painting
- ☐ when I play a game

From *The Adventures of Super3: A Teacher's Guide to Information Literacy for Grades K–2* by Annette C. H. Nelson and Danielle N. DuPuis. Santa Barbara, CA: Linworth. Copyright © 2010.

Name:_____

Madison's Color Chart

Directions: Show Madison what adding two colors together will create.

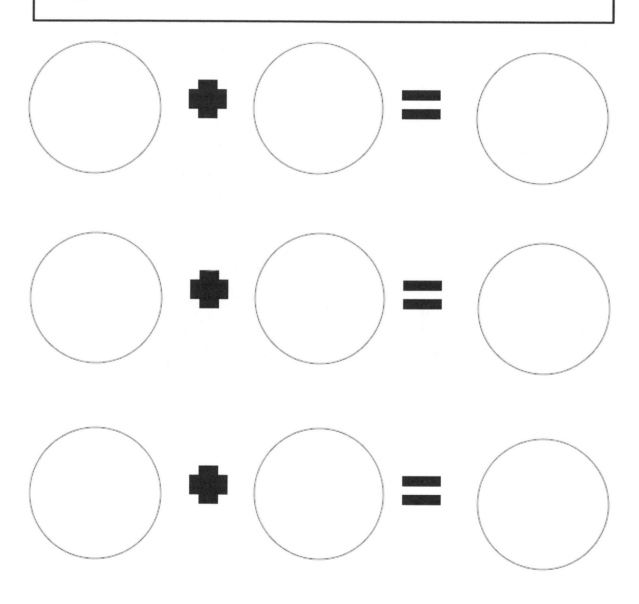

From *The Adventures of Super3: A Teacher's Guide to Information Literacy for Grades K–2* by Annette C. H. Nelson and Danielle N. DuPuis. Santa Barbara, CA: Linworth. Copyright © 2010.

Directions: Print this sheet in color on a blank transparency. Then, cut out each circle to use on your projector.

Name: _____2nd Grade

Color Catastrophe

Problem: Madison needs more colors for her painting. Show her how she can mix colors to make new ones.

Plan

_____

_____

_____

Do

What will you create to solve Madison's Problem?

_____

Review

1. Did you do everything you needed to solve Madison's problem?
_____

2. What did you do a good job on this time?
_____
_____

3. What would you do differently next time? _____
_____

Dear Madison,

_____

_____

_____

_____

_____

You can use this the next time you do an
art project and run out of orange, green,
and purple colors. Have fun creating!

Your friend,

_____

To: Madison Stewart
    6 Color Ct.
    Solution City, MD
         33333

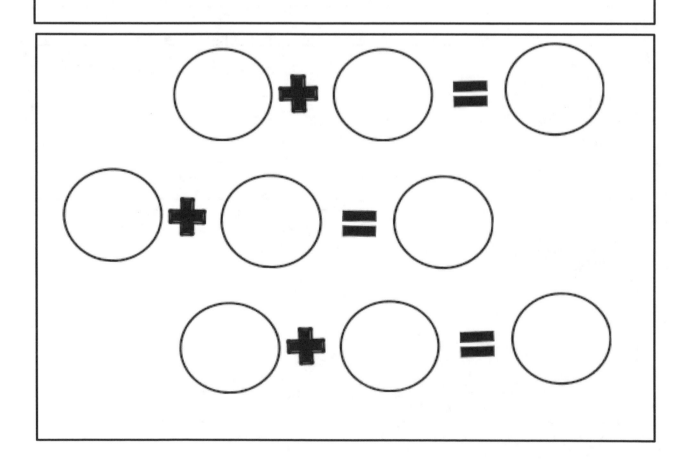

From *The Adventures of Super3: A Teacher's Guide to Information Literacy for Grades K–2* by Annette C. H. Nelson
and Danielle N. DuPuis. Santa Barbara, CA: Linworth. Copyright © 2010.

Lesson 3: Super3 and the First Aid Fix
Performance Objectives

✦ Students will recall the steps of the Super3.

✦ Students will design a plan to solve the problem presented.

✦ Students will create a poster to show the sequence of taking care of a scrape.

✦ Students will review their product and process to determine if they were successful in helping Desiree.

Lesson Timeframe

30 minutes

Provided Materials

✦ Copy of "Super3 and the First Aid Fix" comic (GrKLess3Comic)—Display either a color transparency or electronic PDF version

✦ Copy of "Super3 Step Cards" (Super3StepCards)

✦ Copies for each student of "First Aid Fix" (GrKLess3FirstAidFix)

✦ Copies of "Step Pictures" (GrKLess3Pictures)—one half-sheet per student

Materials You Will Need

✦ Overhead projector or LCD projector and computer

✦ Optional: Document camera

✦ Pencils, crayons, scissors, and glue

Choose one set of materials below:

✦ School health assistant

✦ Nurse costume, soap, cut cream, and bandage

   ✦ Optional: Document camera

✦ First aid books from library or media center

✦ Computers with Internet access to search Web sites on first aid

Engagement

1. Display "Super3 and the First Aid Fix" comic (GrKLess3Comic).

2. Read the comic aloud and ask students what process Super3 should use to help him solve his problem (answer: the Super3).

3. Have students recall the steps of the Super3 and display each step as they name it using the "Super3 Step Cards" (Super3StepCards).

Activity

4. Remind students that when making a plan you list all the possible solutions to the problem before selecting the best one.

5. Ask the students what Desiree should do to fix her cut (visit the school health assistant).

6. Explain that students should make a poster to put on display that shows other students how to take care of cuts.

7. Ask students where they could go for information on how to take care of an injury. Guide students to suggest some of the answers on the plan portion of the "First Aid Fix" (GrKLess3FirstAidFix).

8. Distribute copies of "First Aid Fix" (GrKLess3FirstAidFix) to each student.

9. Look over each suggestion and discuss why it would or would not make the best plan.

10. There are a variety of ways students can find information on how to take proper care of a scrape or cut. As a group, choose the plan that would work best for your class.

   a. Suggested: Ask the school health assistant or nurse to come in and speak with the students about how to take proper care of a cut. This person can demonstrate on a child volunteer or use the "First Aid Cards" (GrKLess3FirstAidCards) to show pictures of what to do.

   b. You or an assistant can pretend to be a nurse and use a student volunteer to demonstrate washing a cut, putting on cut cream, and bandaging it. If you have a document camera you can use it to give the entire class a view of the student volunteer's hand or first aid steps.

   c. You may also choose to read students an easy nonfiction book about first aid and gather information together.

   d. A final option is for students to watch as you navigate a Web site for students about taking care of injuries and discuss the information.

11. Once the students have discovered the information they need, read the "Do" instructions that are on "First Aid Fix" (GrKLess3FirstAidFix).

12. Distribute copies of "Step Pictures" (GrKLess3Pictures), one half-sheet to each child.

13. Allow students time to cut out the pictures of the steps to take care of a cut and glue them in order on the back of their "First Aid Fix" (GrKLess3FirstAidFix).

14. Assist students in reviewing their work by reading and answering the questions on the "Review" portion of "First Aid Fix" (GrKLess3FirstAidFix) as a class.

Closure

15. Ask students to recall who flew in to help Desiree solve her problem (the Super3).

16. Using the "Super3 Step Cards" (Super3StepCards), recall the steps of the Super3 and have students explain what they did for each step.

17. Ask students to recall what they made to help Desiree remember how to care for a cut (a poster).

Assessment

18. Collect and grade "First Aid Fix" (GrKLess3FirstAidFix).

Modifications

For Use with First Grade

✦ Complete the lesson as suggested for kindergarten. However, use the first grade modified worksheet, the "First Aid Fix" (GrKLess3Mod1FirstAidFix). This sheet instructs first graders to make a book instead of a poster. In order to do this they will need copies of the "First Aid Book" (GrKLess3Mod1Book); "Step Pictures" (GrKLess3Pictures), one half-sheet per child; and "Book Captions" (GrKLess3Mod1Captions). To make the book, students need to glue the steps of what should be done to take care of cuts in order, and match the correct caption with the pictures.

For Use with Second Grade

✦ Complete the lesson as suggested for kindergarten. However, use the second grade modified worksheet, the "First Aid Fix" (GrKLess3Mod2FirstAidFix). This sheet instructs second graders to make a book instead of a poster. In order to do this they will need copies of the "First Aid Book" (GrKLess3Mod2Book) and "Step Pictures" (GrKLess3Pictures). To make the book, students will need to glue the steps in order and write captions under each picture describing what to do.

Suggested Books

Clements, Andrew. *Double Trouble in Walla Walla.* Minneapolis: Carolrhoda Books, 1997.

Fluet, Connie. *A Day in the Life of a Nurse.* Mankato, MN: Capstone Press, 2000.

Gordon, Sharon. *Cuts and Scrapes.* New York: Children's Press, 2002.

Palatini, Margie. *Tub-boo-boo.* New York: Simon & Schuster, 2002.

Thaler, Mike. *The School Nurse from the Black Lagoon.* New York: Scholastic, 2009

44

Name: _____Kindergarten

First Aid Fix

Desiree needs to remember how to take care of a cut.

Plan

Make a poster. Underline the best place to find your information for this project.

Use health Web sites to find information.
Read a book about health.
Ask a nurse what you should do.

Do

Cut out, color, and place the first aid steps in order on the back of this worksheet.

Review

Circle your answer to the questions.

Did I do everything I was supposed to do?   Yes   No

Is my work neat?   Yes   No

Did I help Desiree remember how to take care of a cut?   Yes   No

From *The Adventures of Super3: A Teacher's Guide to Information Literacy for Grades K–2* by Annette C. H. Nelson and Danielle N. DuPuis. Santa Barbara, CA: Linworth. Copyright © 2010.

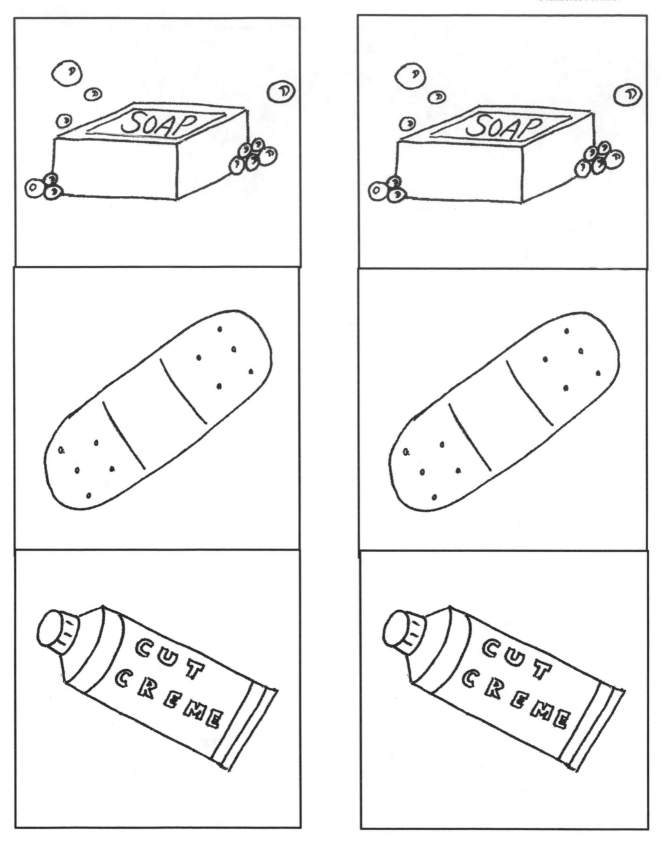

From *The Adventures of Super3: A Teacher's Guide to Information Literacy for Grades K–2* by Annette C. H. Nelson and Danielle N. DuPuis. Santa Barbara, CA: Linworth. Copyright © 2010.

Name: _____ 1st Grade

First Aid Fix

Help Desiree remind others about proper cut care.

Plan

Make a poster. Underline the best place to find your information for this project.

Use health Web sites to find information.

Read a book about health.

Ask a nurse what you should do.

Do

Match the captions with the pictures. Then, put the first aid steps in order to create a book for Desiree.

Review

Circle your answer to the questions.

Did I do everything I was supposed to do?   Yes   No

Is my work neat?   Yes   No

Did I help Desiree remember how to help herself?   Yes   No

From *The Adventures of Super3: A Teacher's Guide to Information Literacy for Grades K–2* by Annette C. H. Nelson and Danielle N. DuPuis. Santa Barbara, CA: Linworth. Copyright © 2010.

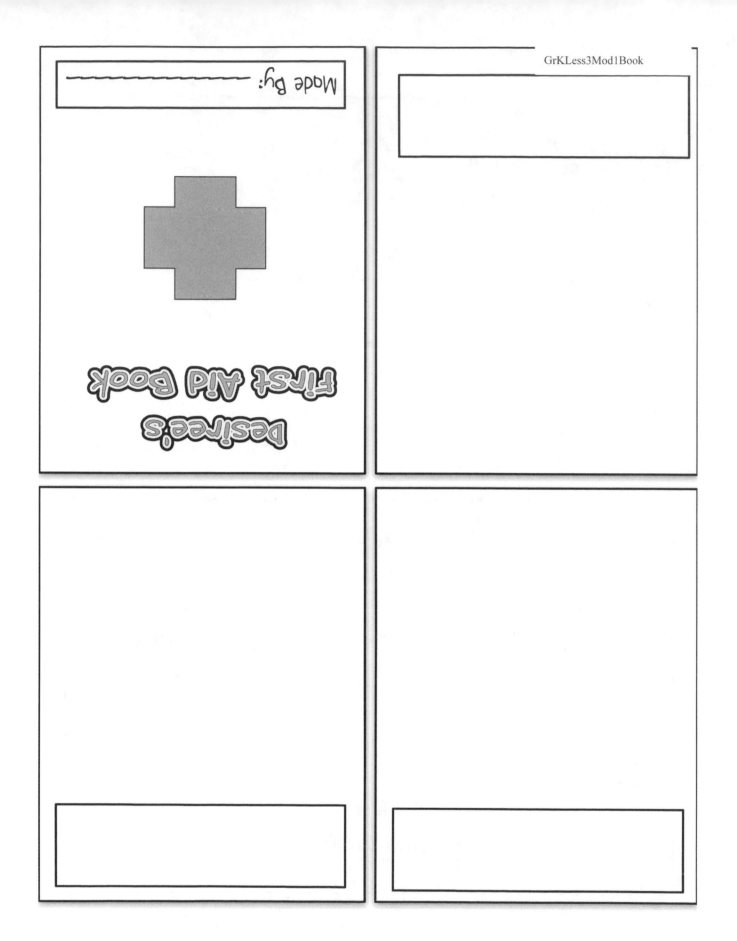

Made By:
_____

Desiree's
First Aid Book

From *The Adventures of Super3: A Teacher's Guide to Information Literacy for Grades K–2* by Annette C. H. Nelson and Danielle N. DuPuis. Santa Barbara, CA: Linworth. Copyright © 2010.

Directions: Cut out the directions in each box to match with the pictures for Desiree's First Aid Book.

Put a bandage over the cut

Wash the area thoroughly

Gently rub on some antibacterial ointment

Directions: Cut out the directions in each box to match with the pictures for Desiree's First Aid Book.

Put a bandage over the cut

Wash the area thoroughly

Gently rub on some antibacterial ointment

Directions: Cut out the directions in each box to match with the pictures for Desiree's First Aid Book.

Put a bandage over the cut

Wash the area thoroughly

Gently rub on some antibacterial ointment

From *The Adventures of Super3: A Teacher's Guide to Information Literacy for Grades K–2* by Annette C. H. Nelson and Danielle N. DuPuis. Santa Barbara, CA: Linworth. Copyright © 2010.

Name: _____ 2nd Grade

First Aid Fix

Desiree needs to remember how to take care of a cut.

Plan

Make a poster. In the spaces below, write the best place to find your information for this project.

_____

_____

_____

Do

Write a caption for the first aid pictures. Then, put the first aid steps in order to create a book for Desiree.

Review

Circle and /or write your answers to the following questions.

Did I do everything I was supposed to do?   Yes   No

Is my work neat?   Yes   No

What skills did I learn? _____

_____

_____

From *The Adventures of Super3: A Teacher's Guide to Information Literacy for Grades K–2* by Annette C. H. Nelson and Danielle N. DuPuis. Santa Barbara, CA: Linworth. Copyright © 2010.

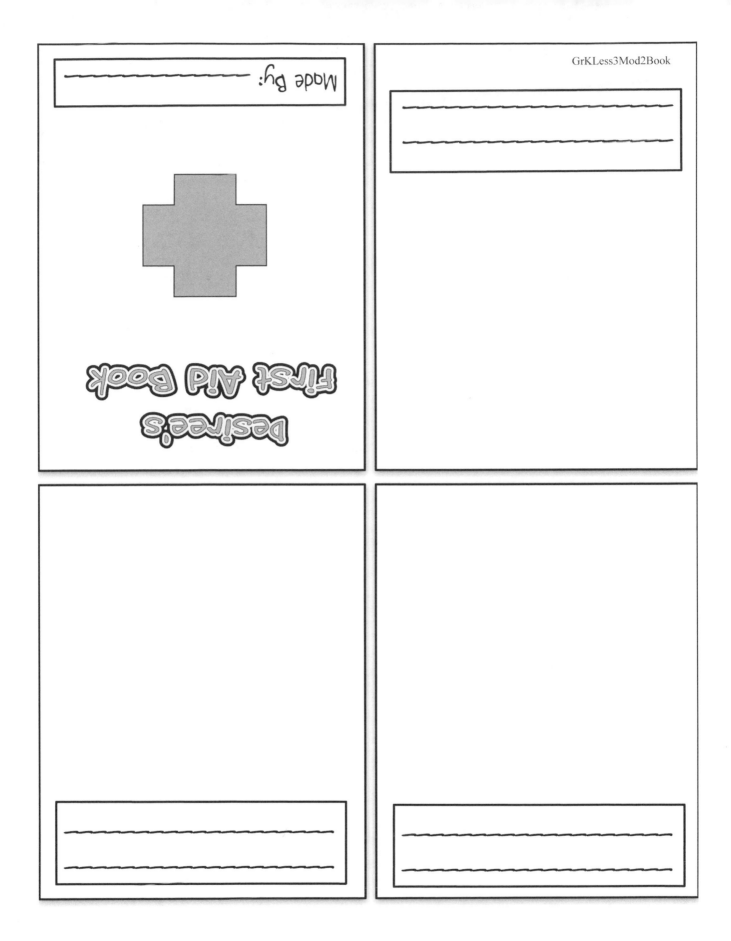

Made By:

Desiree's First Aid Book

From *The Adventures of Super3: A Teacher's Guide to Information Literacy for Grades K–2* by Annette C. H. Nelson and Danielle N. DuPuis. Santa Barbara, CA: Linworth. Copyright © 2010.

CHAPTER 3

Super3 for First Grade

First graders present an interesting challenge for teachers and teacher-librarians. They need to solve in-depth problems but often need support in order to do so. First graders enjoy working with the Super3 and are able to apply the strategy to more academically focused problems.

The three first grade lessons found here begin with Super3 encountering an unfamiliar word in "Super3 and the Mysterious Word." He overhears a student reading but does not know the meaning of one of the words. The students have to help Super3 look up the word in a dictionary to find its meaning. Students can then practice their context clue skills and determine the meaning of other unfamiliar words within several sentences. In the second lesson, "Super3 and the Perfect Pet," Vijay is upset because he doesn't know how to find the perfect pet for his family. Students have to determine his needs, select a pet from the pet-shop flyer, and write a postcard to Vijay explaining their choice. The third lesson, "Super3 and the Snack Attack," incorporates the idea of text features in nonfiction text with the common problem of wanting a snack. Kyra is hungry but it's too early for dinner. First graders need to help her figure out a snack to make using Super3's own cookbook. Once they determine a good snack choice for Kyra based on her kitchen supplies, they investigate the concept of text features through a PowerPoint game.

These educational and exciting first grade lessons will provide students with examples of the Super3 process in use. The guided practice will help them understand how to use plan, do, and review independently.

Lesson 1: Super3 and the Mysterious Word
Performance Objectives

✦ Students will name the steps of the Super3.

✦ Students will apply the Super3 process to determine the meaning of an unfamiliar word.

✦ Students will use a dictionary to find and record the meaning of the word "ravenous."

Lesson Timeframe

30 minutes

Provided Materials

✦ Copy of "Super3 and the Mysterious Word" comic (Gr1Less1Comic)—Display either a color transparency or electronic PDF version

✦ Copy of "Super3 Step Cards" (Super3StepCards)

✦ Copies for each student of "Super3's Mysterious Word" (Gr1Less1MysteriousWord)

✦ Copies for each student of "Super3's Vivid Vocabulary" (Gr1Less1VividVocab)

✦ Copies of assembled "OED: One Extreme Dictionary" (Gr1Less1Dictionary), one for each pair of students

✦ Optional: Copy of "Super3 Sort" (Gr1Less1Sort)

Materials You Will Need

✦ Overhead projector or LCD projector and computer

✦ Optional: Document camera

✦ Pencils

✦ Timer

Engagement

1. Display a copy of "Super3 and the Mysterious Word" comic (Gr1Less1Comic).

2. Read the comic aloud and ask students what process Super3 should use to help him solve his problem (answer: the Super3).

3. Have students recall the steps of the Super3. Display each step as it is named by using the "Super3 Step Cards" (Super3StepCards).

Activity

4. Ask students to pretend they are the Super3 and it is their job to solve the problem of the mysterious word.

5. Instruct students to think-pair-share about their plan. First, students need to think independently for 30 seconds about a plan for the problem. Next, students pair up with a person next to them for 30 seconds and discuss what they thought. Finally, ask students to share their ideas with the whole class.

6. Record student ideas for the plan and write these on the board. If needed, give guidance to help students think of the options on the "Super3's Mysterious Word" worksheet (Gr1Less1MysteriousWord).

7. Distribute copies of "Super3's Mysterious Word" (Gr1Less1MysteriousWord) to each student.

8. Project a copy of "Super3's Mysterious Word" and assist students in reading the directions.

9. Discuss as a class the best solution to the problem (answer: looking the word up in a dictionary). Instruct students to circle the best answer.

10. Explain to the students that they will now complete the next step of the Super3 and "do" their plan.

11. Distribute copies of "OED: One Extreme Dictionary" (Gr1Less1Dictionary) to each pair of students.

12. Review how to use a dictionary to find words. It might be helpful to have the alphabet on display so students see in which direction they need to turn pages to find the word "ravenous." If you have access to a document camera, use it to show students how to use a dictionary. Point out how to use the guide words at the top of each dictionary page.

13. Allow students time to look up the word "ravenous" in the dictionary. Once the definition has been found, have students write the meaning of the word in the "Do" box on "Super3's Mysterious Word" (Gr1Less1MysteriousWord).

14. Instruct students to complete the last step of the Super3 in order to "Review." Assist when needed by reading the questions and helping them circle the correct answers.

15. Explain to students that Super3 was so excited about learning the meaning of the word "ravenous" that he looked up more words in the dictionary.

16. Distribute copies of "Super3's Vivid Vocabulary" (Gr1Less1VividVocab) and allow students time to use their context clue skills to determine the meaning of each word.

Optional

Explain how to play the "Super3 Sort" (Super3Sort) game and play the game with the students.

Closure

17. Gather students back together and ask students to recall the three steps of the Super3 and explain how they used the steps to solve the mysterious word problem.

Assessment

18. Collect both the "Super3's Mysterious Word" (Gr1Less1MysteriousWord) and "Super3's Vivid Vocabulary" (Gr1Less1VividVocab) and grade.

19. Take anecdotal observations of student answer choices during the "Super3 Sort" (Gr1Less1Sort) game.

Modifications

For Use with Kindergarten

✦ Have the teacher or teacher-librarian demonstrate looking up the word in the dictionary instead of having students look up the word.

✦ Use the kindergarten modified version of "Super3's Mysterious Word" (Gr1Less1ModKMysteriousWord).

✦ Display a copy of "Super3's Vivid Vocabulary" (Gr1Less1VividVocab) and complete aloud as a class.

For Use with Second Grade

✦ Use the second grade modified version of "Super3's Mysterious Word" (Gr1Less1Mod2MysteriousWord).

✦ To make this lesson more challenging, use a student dictionary that contains the word "ravenous" instead of the "OED: One Extreme Dictionary" (Gr1Less1Dictionary).

✦ You may also wish to have students use one of the words from the "OED: One Extreme Dictionary" (Gr1Less1Dictionary) in a sentence.

Suggested Books

Banks, Kate. *Max's Words*. New York: Farrar, Straus and Giroux, 2006.

Curtis, Jamie Lee. *Big Words for Little People*. New York: Joanna Colter, 2008.

O'Connor, Jane. *Fancy Nancy*. New York: HarperCollins, 2006.

Rappaport, Doreen. *Abe's Honest Words: The Life of Abraham Lincoln*. New York: Hyperion, 2009.

Rappaport, Doreen. *Martin's Big Words: the Life of Dr. Martin Luther King Jr.* New York: Hyperion, 2007.

Schotter, Roni. *The Boy Who Loved Words*. New York: Schwartz & Wade Books, 2006.

SUPER3 GOES OUT INTO THE WORLD TO TRY AND SOLVE HIS FIRST PROBLEM!

DUN DUN DA DA!!

SUPER3 FLIES OVER BUILDINGS AND LANDS IN A LIBRARY

SOMEONE AROUND HERE HAS TO HAVE A PROBLEM! I WONDER WHO I CAN HELP?

SUPER3 LISTENS IN ON A BOY READING A BOOK.

THE RAVENOUS DINOSAUR WAS ABOUT TO ATTACK THE SMALL LIZARD.

RAVENOUS!? WHAT DOES THAT MEAN!?

SUDDENLY, SUPER3 REALIZES HE HAS A PROBLEM! HE HAS NO IDEA WHAT THE WORD RAVENOUS MEANS.

TO BE CONTINUED...

Name: _____1st grade

Super3's Mysterious Word

Problem: Super3 doesn't know what the word "ravenous" means.

Plan

Circle the best plan that you will do.

1. Ask a friend.

2. Look up the word in the dictionary.

3. Look on the word wall.

4. Ask a teacher.

Do

Write the meaning of the word.

Ravenous: _____

_____

_____

_____

Review

Circle Yes or No to answer each question.

Is my job done?   Yes   No

Did I do what I was supposed to do?
                         Yes   No

Should I do something before I turn it in?
                         Yes   No

From *The Adventures of Super3: A Teacher's Guide to Information Literacy for Grades K–2* by Annette C. H. Nelson and Danielle N. DuPuis. Santa Barbara, CA: Linworth. Copyright © 2010.

Name:_____1st Grade

Super3's Vivid Vocabulary

Super3 was so excited about finding the word "ravenous" he looked up more words in the dictionary. Use the sentences to figure out what the words mean.

The gigantic watermelon was so huge Super3 couldn't finish eating it!

Gigantic means:_____

The hilarious clown made Super3 laugh so hard he spit out his milk!

Hilarious means:_____

Super3 used to be terrified of the dark but sleeping with a night light helps him to be less afraid.

Terrified means:_____

Super3 helped dry the tears of the sobbing girl who fell and scraped her leg.

Sobbing means:_____

From *The Adventures of Super3: A Teacher's Guide to Information Literacy for Grades K–2* by Annette C. H. Nelson and Danielle N. DuPuis. Santa Barbara, CA: Linworth. Copyright © 2010.

DIRECTIONS:

TO MAKE ONE DICTIONARY:

1. COPY THE PAGES ON CARD STOCK AND LAMINATE IF DESIRED

2. CUT OUT EACH PAGE.

3. BIND TOGETHER LIKE A BOOK USING A STAPLER OR A BINDING COMB AND BINDING MACHINE.

OED: One Extreme Dictionary

EXCITING WORDS TO JAZZ THINGS UP!

Abundant   Entomologist

abundant: lots of something

adore: to love something

adventure: an exciting experience

balderdash: something that doesn't make sense

bamboozle: to trick someone

cacophony: loud noise--normally annoying

captive: someone's prisoner

delicious: really yummy

directions: tell you how to do something

entomologist: a scientist who studies insects   1

Fearless   Jamboree

fearless: brave

frigid: really cold

gigantic: really big

glisten: to shine

habitat: the place where something lives

hilarious: really funny

independent: doing something without help

invincible: unable to be hurt

jamboree: a big, noisy, fun party   2

From *The Adventures of Super3: A Teacher's Guide to Information Literacy for Grades K–2* by Annette C. H. Nelson and Danielle N. DuPuis. Santa Barbara, CA: Linworth. Copyright © 2010.

Journey   Oblivious

journey: a trip

kind: nice

labyrinth: a maze

literate: to be able to read

massive: really big

mystery: something that can't be explained

naughty: bad

nincompoop: a silly person

oblivious: unaware or clueless

3

Odor   Superb

odor: a smell

petrify: to scare someone so they can't move

polar bear: a large white bear who lives in the North
            Pole and Arctic Circle area

quagmire: a large problem

quarrel: a fight

ravenous: very hungry or very greedy

ruckus: a lot of noise

sage: a wise or smart person

superb: wonderful

4

Terrific   Zany

terrific: wonderful

terrified: really scared

umbrella: a tool to keep you dry when it's raining

unusual: strange

victory: winning

volunteer: to say you will do something without being
           asked to do it

weeping: crying

whiz: someone who is good at something

zany: silly

5

From *The Adventures of Super3: A Teacher's Guide to Information Literacy for Grades K–2* by Annette C. H. Nelson
and Danielle N. DuPuis. Santa Barbara, CA: Linworth. Copyright © 2010.

Super3 Sort

Preparation: Using the "Super3 Step Cards" (Super3StepCards), label three areas of your room with, "Plan," "Do," and "Review."

Activity: Read the following situations aloud to your class. After reading each situation, ask your students to move to the part of the room that is labeled with the appropriate Super3 step. You can get creative about having your students move. They can hop, crab walk, tiptoe, or use some other step to make it more fun. Be sure to let students know the correct answer before moving on to the next situation.

Situation 1: Alex double-checks his math homework before turning it in to his teacher.
> Super3 Step: Review

Situation 2: Emily walks her dog.
> Super3 Step: Do

Situation 3: Christopher thinks about how he wants to rearrange his room.
> Super3 Step: Plan

Situation 4: Jody shares a toy with her sister.
> Super3 Step: Do

Situation 5: Kareem thinks about whom he wants to invite to his birthday party and makes a list of friends.
> Super3 Step: Plan

Situation 6: Mi'a goes over her spelling test before handing it in.
> Super3 Step: Review

Situation 7: Justin plays basketball with his friend, Sam.
> Super3 Step: Do

Situation 8: After planting a tree in her backyard, Maria looks at the tree and says, "I did everything I was supposed to do! I did a really great job!"
> Super3 Step: Review

Situation 9: Kevin goes ice-skating with his friend.
> Super3 Step: Do

Situation 10: Molly thinks she will look in her classroom or her book bag for her lost lunch box.
> Super3 Step: Plan.

From *The Adventures of Super3: A Teacher's Guide to Information Literacy for Grades K–2* by Annette C. H. Nelson and Danielle N. DuPuis. Santa Barbara, CA: Linworth. Copyright © 2010.

Name: _____Kindergarten

Super3's Mysterious Word

Problem: Super3 doesn't know what the word "ravenous" means.

Plan

Circle the best plan that you will do.

1. Ask a friend.

2. Look up the word in the dictionary.

3. Look on the word wall.

4. Ask a teacher.

Do

Circle the correct meaning of the word ravenous.

Ravenous:

1. Very hungry

2. Happy

3. Mad

Review
Circle Yes or No to answer each question.

Is my job done?   Yes   No

Did I do what I was supposed to do?
                          Yes   No

Should I do something before I turn it in?
                          Yes   No

From *The Adventures of Super3: A Teacher's Guide to Information Literacy for Grades K–2* by Annette C. H. Nelson and Danielle N. DuPuis. Santa Barbara, CA: Linworth. Copyright © 2010.

Name: _____2nd grade

Super3's Mysterious Word

Problem: Super3 doesn't know what the word "ravenous" means.

Plan

List where you can find your information.

1. _____

2. _____

3. _____

4. _____

Circle the best one.

Do

Write the meaning of the word.

Ravenous: _____

_____

_____

_____

_____

Review

Circle Yes or No to answer each question.

Is my job done?   Yes   No

Did I do what I was supposed to do?
                         Yes   No

Should I do something before I turn it in?   Yes   No

From *The Adventures of Super3: A Teacher's Guide to Information Literacy for Grades K–2* by Annette C. H. Nelson and Danielle N. DuPuis. Santa Barbara, CA: Linworth. Copyright © 2010.

Lesson 2: Super3 and the Perfect Pet
Performance Objectives

✦ Students will analyze information to determine the perfect pet for Vijay.

✦ Students will compose a postcard for Vijay, naming reasons for their suggested pet.

✦ Students will evaluate their product and process when finished.

Lesson Timeframe

40 minutes

Provided Materials

✦ Copy of "Super3 and the Perfect Pet" comic (Gr1Less2Comic)—Display either a color transparency or electronic PDF version

✦ Copy of "Super3 Step Cards" (Super3StepCards)

✦ Copy of "Pet Plan Cards" (Gr1Less2PlanCards)

✦ Copies for each student of "*Paws-itively Pets*" (Gr1Less2PetFlyer) (you may wish to copy these in color, back to back on 11x14 paper to make it look more like a newspaper flyer insert)

✦ Copies for each student of "Postcard" (Gr1Less2Postcard)—one half-sheet per student

✦ Copy of "Let's Review" (Gr1Less2Review) to display using transparency or an electronic copy

Materials You Will Need

✦ Overhead projector or LCD projector and computer

✦ One newspaper with flyers inside

✦ Optional: Document camera

✦ Pencils

✦ Crayons

Engagement

1. Pretend to read the newspaper to yourself and have the flyers fall out of it as you read. Mention to the students that these flyers are sometimes helpful when you need to buy something.

2. Display a copy of "Super3 and the Perfect Pet" comic (Gr1Less2Comic).

3. Read the comic to the students and ask them what process Super3 should use to help him solve his problem (answer: the Super3).

4. Have students recall the steps of the Super3. Display each step as it is named by using the "Super3 Step Cards" (Super3StepCards).

Activity

5. Explain to students that they need to help Super3 and Vijay figure out what pet from *Paws-itively Pets* would be best for him. Ask students to think of ways to determine a furless, unique pet that is under $100 and would be for sale at *Paws-itively Pets*.

6. Record student ideas for the plan. If needed, give guidance to help students think of options such as: asking a friend what pet is the best, going to the pet store, reading a book about pets, reading a Web site about pets, looking at the flyer from *Paws-itively Pets*. You can hold up the newspaper flyers from the beginning of the class to help students think of the idea of looking in a flyer.

7. As a class, choose the best option for the plan (looking at the store flyer).

8. Ask students to think about what they could create to inform Vijay of their suggested pet. Write down the suggestions on the board and pick the best one (suggested: write Vijay a postcard and "mail" it to him).

9. Use the "Pet Plan Cards" (Gr1Less2PlanCards) to display the steps of the plan on the board. Refer to the plan as you "do" each step.

10. Explain to students that they will now complete the next step of the Super3 and "do" their plan.

11. Distribute copies of "*Paws-itively Pets*" (Gr1Less2PetFlyer) to each student or pair of students.

12. Display a copy "*Paws-itively Pets*" (Gr1Less2PetFlyer) and assist students in reading the descriptions of the pets.

13. Have students individually pick a pet for Vijay. Remind them that the pet needs to be under $100, furless, and unique (correct possibilities include: frog, gecko, cockatiel).

14. Display a copy of "Dear Vijay" (Gr1Less1Postcard) and demonstrate how to write a post-card to Vijay. Make sure to include the type of pet he should choose and why.

15. Distribute copies of "Dear Vijay" (Gr1Less1Postcard) to each student and instruct them to write their own postcard. Explain how to write the paragraph to Vijay on one side and draw a picture of the pet on the back where the picture would normally go on a postcard.

Closure

16. Once students finish, project a transparency or electronic copy of "Let's Review" (Gr1Less2Review) and review the product and problem-solving process with the students.

17. Ask students to recall who flew in to help Vijay solve his problem (the Super3) and what the three steps of the Super3 are called (plan, do, review).

Assessment

18. Collect and grade copies of "Dear Vijay" (Gr1Less1Postcard).

Modifications

For Use with Kindergarten

✦ Have the teacher or teacher-librarian read and display only the first page of the "*Paws-itively Pets*" flyer (Gr1Less2PetFlyer) to the students. Discuss as a class the perfect pet for Vijay and decide together which one he should pick and why.

✦ Use the kindergarten modified version of the "Postcard" (Gr1Less2ModKPostcard). Using the postcard pictures on the second page, have students cut out the picture of the pet they selected and the reasons why this is the best pet for Vijay to get and glue them on the postcard in the appropriate places.

For Use with Second Grade

✦ Use the second grade modified version of the "Postcard" (Gr1Less2ModGr2Postcard). Depending on the reading level of your students, they may independently read the "*Paws-itively Pets*" (Gr1Less2PetFlyer) and decide their pet choice.

Suggested Books

Bennett, Kelly. *Not Norman: A Goldfish Story*. Cambridge, MA: Candlewick Press, 2005.

Graham, Bob. *Let's Get a Pup!* London: Walker, 2001.

O'Connor, Jane. *Fancy Nancy and the Posh Puppy*. New York: HarperCollins, 2007.

Orloff, Karen Kaufman. *I Wanna Iguana*. New York: Putnam, 2004.

Willems, Mo. *The Pigeon Wants a Puppy!* New York: Hyperion, 2008.

Less than $100

No fur

Choose the perfect pet for Vijay

Read the Paws–itively Pets Flyer

PET PLAN CARDS: COPY ON CARDSTOCK, CUT OUT, AND LAMINATE. THEN USE TO DISPLAY THE PLAN FOR THE STUDENTS.

 From *The Adventures of Super3: A Teacher's Guide to Information Literacy for Grades K–2* by Annette C. H. Nelson and Danielle N. DuPuis. Santa Barbara, CA: Linworth. Copyright © 2010.

Gr1Less2PlanCards Cont.

Make a postcard for Vijay telling the pet you chose and why

Unique

From *The Adventures of Super3: A Teacher's Guide to Information Literacy for Grades K–2* by Annette C. H. Nelson and Danielle N. DuPuis. Santa Barbara, CA: Linworth. Copyright © 2010.

Paws-itively Pets
The perfect pet store!

gecko

This adorable green gecko is the perfect pet. Feed him a couple of crickets every few days, and he's good to go. Doesn't require a lot of extra care and is very friendly.

Cost: $2.5

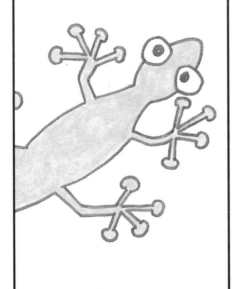

Hamster

These adorable little furballs are great pets. They require little care, but are great fun to watch! Purchase a tunnel tank to go along with your new hamster to really have a ball!

Cost: $12

Calico Kitten

This adorable kitten is black, white, and orange. This common breed of cat is perfect for anyone who loves to snuggle up with a fluffy and furry animal. We have many of this gorgeous kittens for sale. Please come take a look.

Cost: A bargain price of only $7.5!

From *The Adventures of Super3: A Teacher's Guide to Information Literacy for Grades K–2* by Annette C. H. Nelson and Danielle N. DuPuis. Santa Barbara, CA: Linworth. Copyright © 2010.

DALMATION

Known to some as the Fire house dog, this spotted friend is an extremely loyal pet. He is an 8 week old puppy and requires a lot of exercise and attention. Perfect for families, he loves children.

Cost: $225

Frog

Frogs make nice pets. They are amphibians and love spending time in areas that are moist. Before purchasing this pet, make sure you have the proper cage so that you can recreate a healthy habitat for your new frog. A very unique pet!

Cost $18

Goldfish

Extremely easy to take care of. This common house pet is great to have around to look at. Fish can't live out of water, so he'll need to stay in a fish bowl full of water. Goldfish aren't known to do all that much, but they are fun to look at!

Cost: $1.95

From *The Adventures of Super3: A Teacher's Guide to Information Literacy for Grades K–2* by Annette C. H. Nelson and Danielle N. DuPuis. Santa Barbara, CA: Linworth. Copyright © 2010.

Ferret

These furry creatures are very cat-like. They are litter box trained and can live in or out of a cage. Very fun and unique! Bathe this pet weekly to cut down on unnecessary odors.

Cost $98

Cockatiel

This bird is a great pet to have! It has been hand raised, so you can hold and pet it. This cockatiel can even talk. Amaze your friends and family with this creature's marvelous talents! A fairly low maintenance pet. Likes to eat seeds, fruits, and vegetables. Will require a medium sized bird cage.

Cost: $ 75

From *The Adventures of Super3: A Teacher's Guide to Information Literacy for Grades K–2* by Annette C. H. Nelson and Danielle N. DuPuis. Santa Barbara, CA: Linworth. Copyright © 2010.

Dear Vijay,

You should get a _____ for
a pet because _____
_____
_____
_____
_____

I hope you have fun with your new pet!
Congratulations on your report card!

Your friend,

_____

To: Vijay Patel
3 Problem Place
Solution City, MD
33333

Dear Vijay,

You should get a _____ for
a pet because _____
_____
_____
_____
_____

I hope you have fun with your new pet!
Congratulations on your report card!

Your friend,

_____

To: Vijay Patel
3 Problem Place
Solution City, MD
33333

From *The Adventures of Super3: A Teacher's Guide to Information Literacy for Grades K–2* by Annette C. H. Nelson and Danielle N. DuPuis. Santa Barbara, CA: Linworth. Copyright © 2010.

Let's Review

Think about the Postcard you made:

☐ Did you do and include everything that was required?

☐ Is your work neat?

☐ Did you sign your name on the postcard?

☐ Would you be proud for anyone to view this work?

Think about how you solved the problem:

What did you do well this time?

What would you do differently next time?

How could you use Super3 to help you solve another problem?

From *The Adventures of Super3: A Teacher's Guide to Information Literacy for Grades K–2* by Annette C. H. Nelson and Danielle N. DuPuis. Santa Barbara, CA: Linworth. Copyright © 2010.

Dear Vijay,

You should get a

because

and

Your friend,

_____

To: Vijay Patel
3 Problem Place
Solution City, MD
33333

Directions:

Carefully select the pet on the right that Vijay should choose from the pet store. Cut it out and paste it onto your postcard. Next, select the two best reasons from the 8 listed below as to why this is the best pet for Vijay to get.

it barks	more than $ 100		
has feathers	less than $ 100		
sheds a LOT	everyone has this kind of pet		
FUR	This pet is unique!		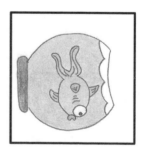

From *The Adventures of Super3: A Teacher's Guide to Information Literacy for Grades K–2* by Annette C. H. Nelson and Danielle N. DuPuis. Santa Barbara, CA: Linworth. Copyright © 2010.

Dear Vijay,

_____
_____
_____
_____
_____
_____

To: Vijay Patel
3 Problem Place
Solution City, MD
33333

Your friend,

_____

Dear Vijay,

_____
_____
_____
_____
_____
_____

To: Vijay Patel
3 Problem Place
Solution City, MD
33333

Your friend,

_____

From *The Adventures of Super3: A Teacher's Guide to Information Literacy for Grades K–2* by Annette C. H. Nelson and Danielle N. DuPuis. Santa Barbara, CA: Linworth. Copyright © 2010.

Lesson 3: Super3 and the Snack Attack
Performance Objectives

- ✦ Students will design a plan to solve the problem presented.
- ✦ Students will identify a snack Kyra can make based on supplies available.
- ✦ Students will cite the source of their information.

Lesson Timeframe

40 minutes

Provided Materials

- ✦ Copy of "Super3 and the Snack Attack" comic (Gr1Less3Comic)—Display either a color transparency or electronic PDF version
- ✦ Copy of "Super3 Step Cards" (Super3StepCards)
- ✦ Copies for each student of "Snack Attack" (Gr1Less3SnackAttack)
- ✦ Copies of "Super Snacks" (Gr1Less3SuperSnacks)
- ✦ Copy of "Kyra's Refrigerator" (Gr1Less3Refrigerator)
- ✦ Copy of "Kyra's Cabinet" (Gr1Less3Cabinet)
- ✦ Optional: PowerPoint Game "Text Feature Teacher" (Gr1Less3TextFeature)

Materials You Will Need

- ✦ Overhead projector or LCD projector and computer
- ✦ Pencils

Preparation Before Lesson

Copy and assemble copies of the "Super Snacks" Cookbook (Gr1Less3SuperSnacks) for each pair of students. If you have a binding machine you can use this to assemble the cookbooks. You may also wish to gather children's cookbooks for students to search in addition to or instead of the "Super Snacks" Cookbook.

Engagement

1. Display a copy of "Super3 and the Snack Attack" comic (Gr1Less3Comic).
2. Read the comic aloud and ask students what process Kyra should use to help her solve her problem (answer: the Super3).
3. Have students recall the steps of the Super3. Display each step as it is named by using the "Super3 Step Cards" (Super3StepCards).

Activity

4. Explain to students that they need to solve the problem and help Kyra use the Super3 to find a snack.

5. Instruct students to think about where Kyra could find or make a snack. Give students time to think of a plan on their own, then time to discuss with the people sitting near them, and finally, time to share their ideas with the class.

6. As students come up with ideas, write each one on the board. Possible suggestions include: go to the store and buy a snack, make a snack at home, or go to a neighbor and ask for a snack.

7. Guide students to decide that making a snack is the best option because Kyra is too young to go to the store or her neighbor's by herself.

8. Distribute copies of "Snack Attack" (Gr1Less3SnackAttack) to each student.

9. Project a transparency or electronic copy of the worksheet and assist students in reading the directions.

10. Discuss the different options for finding a snack recipe and discuss positives and negatives for each possible plan.

    - look in a cookbook

    - call a friend

    - ask an adult for help

    - look for a recipe on the Internet

11. Choose a plan as a class and have students record it on their worksheet. It is suggested that students look in a cookbook (you may choose to gather cookbooks from your library's collection, or use the provided "Super Snacks" Cookbook (Gr1Less3SuperSnacks)).

12. Display the pictures of "Kyra's Refrigerator" (Gr1Less3Refrigerator) and "Kyra's Cabinet" (Gr1Less3Cabinet). Tell students to make sure Kyra has the proper ingredients in order to make a snack they find in one of the cookbooks.

13. Move on to the "Do" step and have students look for a recipe using the cookbooks provided.

14. Once students find a snack for Kyra to make, instruct them to record the source, page number, and title of the recipe in the "Do" section of "Snack Attack" (Gr1Less3SnackAttack).

15. Assist students in reviewing their work by reading the "Review" section of the displayed "Snack Attack" (Gr1Less3SnackAttack).

16. Collect the "Snack Attack" (Gr1Less3SnackAttack).

Optional

Explain to students that authors try to make nonfiction books easier to understand by using text features. Explain that cookbooks use a lot of great text features.

Show and play the PowerPoint "Text Feature Teacher" (Gr1Less3TextFeature) with the students. *Note:* You will need to have the PowerPoint on Slide Show view in order for the game to work properly. If you have the equipment, you can also have each child play this game independently or in pairs on their own computers.

Closure

17. Gather students back together and ask students to recall the three steps of the Super3 and explain how they used the steps to solve Kyra's snack attack problem.

Assessment

18. Collect and grade the "Snack Attack" (Gr1Less3SnackAttack).

Modifications

For Use with Kindergarten

✦ Use the kindergarten modified version of "Snack Attack" (Gr1Less3ModKSnackAttack).

✦ Only use "Super Snacks" (Gr1Less3SuperSnacks) to search for recipes instead of other cookbooks. You may also wish to display this cookbook as well as distributing copies so that students can easily follow along as you read.

✦ Instead of the optional PowerPoint Game, you may wish to have students graph their favorite snack. Project an electronic copy of "Our Favorite Snack" (Gr1Less3ModKFavoriteSnack) or use chart paper to make the graph. Let students make their own paper Super3 and tape their Super3 to the graph under the snack they would like best.

For Use with Second Grade

✦ Use the second grade modified version of "Snack Attack" (Gr1Less3Mod2SnackAttack).

✦ Instruct students to find a snack recipe on the Internet instead of using the provided cookbook. Some suggested Web sites to bookmark for this part of the lesson are:

  ✦ *Allrecipes,* http://allrecipes.com/.

  ✦ "Recipes," *Kids Health*, Nemours Foundation, http://kidshealth.org/kid/recipes/.

  ✦ "Snack Time," *Family Fun*, http://familyfun.go.com/recipes/kids/specialfeature/recipes-snacks/.

✦ Play the PowerPoint Game "Text Feature Teacher" (Gr1Less3TextFeature) with the students and discuss the text features that many nonfiction books, including cookbooks, use to help readers understand the text.

Suggested Books

Elffers, Joost, and Saxton Freymann. *Fast Food.* New York: Arthur A. Levine Books, 2006.

McFarland, Lyn Rossiter. *Mouse Went Out to Get a Snack.* New York: Farrar, Straus and Giroux, 2005.

Numeroff, Laura. *If You Give a Cat a Cupcake.* New York: Harper Collins, 2008.

Rocklin, Joanne. *One Hungry Cat.* New York: Scholastic, 1997.

Stevens, Janet. *Cook-a-doodle-doo!* San Diego: Harcourt Brace, 1999.

Sturges, Philemon, and Amy Walrod. *The Little Red Hen (Makes a Pizza).* New York: Puffin, 2002.

Name: _____ 1st Grade

Snack Attack!

Problem: Kyra is hungry but can't have dinner until 6:30p.m.

Plan

Check off the box that shows your plan.

☐ Ask an adult for help   ☐ Call a friend

☐ Look in a cookbook   ☐ Look for a recipe on the Internet

Do

What should Kyra make?

_____

List the ingredients Kyra will need to make her snack.

_____

_____

Review

Circle Yes or No to answer each question.

Did I do everything I was supposed to do?

Yes   No

Did I choose a recipe for Kyra to make and list the ingredients she will need?

Yes   No

From *The Adventures of Super3: A Teacher's Guide to Information Literacy for Grades K–2* by Annette C. H. Nelson and Danielle N. DuPuis. Santa Barbara, CA: Linworth. Copyright © 2010.

$2.95

Super Snacks for Super Kids By Super3

Flying Saucers

Ingredients:
round crackers
tomato sauce
shredded cheese

Using a teaspoon, spread a little tomato sauce on a round cracker. Sprinkle a little shredded cheese on top of the saucy cracker. Your mini pizza is complete!

Ants on a Log

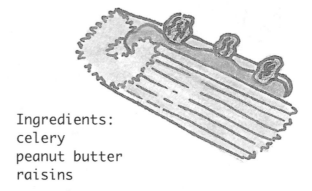

Ingredients:
celery
peanut butter
raisins

Using a butter knife, smear some peanut butter into the valley of the celery. Place the raisins into the peanut butter. You now have a delicious snack! Mmm.... those ants look good!

Popcorn

Ingredients:
1 cup of popcorn kernels
1 brown paper lunch bag

Place a cup of popcorn kernels into a brown paper bag. Fold the top of the bag over several times. Place in the microwave and cook for 2 minutes. When you hear the popcorn stop popping, open your bag. Mmmm... now you have a bag of nice warm popcorn!

Banana Burgers

Ingredients:
1 banana
6 mini rice cakes
peanut butter

First, spread peanut butter on one side of each mini rice cake. After peeling the banana, slice it until you have several circular pieces. Place a piece of banana onto 3 of the mini rice cakes. Top each rice cake and banana with another rice cake. In just a few minutes, you have 3 banana burgers ready to eat!

Trail Mix

Ingredients:
1/2 cup of cereal
1 Tbsp almonds
1 Tbsp peanuts
1 Tbsp small bite
  sized chocolate candy

Place 1/2 cup of cereal into a bowl. Next, add in 1 Tbsp of almonds, 1 Tbsp of peanuts, and 1 Tbsp of chocolate candy. Mix with a spoon until the mix is blended together. It is now ready to eat! Substitute dry fruit instead of the chocolate to make this snack even more healthy.

Fruit Kabobs

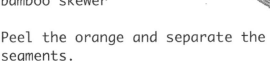

Ingredients:
1 orange
3 cheese cubes
2 strawberries
3 grapes
bamboo skewer

Peel the orange and separate the segments.
Poke your skewer through one of the segments. In no particular order, alternate the other pieces of fruit and cheese. Once your skewer is packed with fruit and cheese, your Fruit Skewer is complete and ready to eat!

From *The Adventures of Super3: A Teacher's Guide to Information Literacy for Grades K–2* by Annette C. H. Nelson and Danielle N. DuPuis. Santa Barbara, CA: Linworth. Copyright © 2010.

From *The Adventures of Super3: A Teacher's Guide to Information Literacy for Grades K–2* by Annette C. H. Nelson and Danielle N. DuPuis. Santa Barbara, CA: Linworth. Copyright © 2010.

Gr1Less3Cabinet

From *The Adventures of Super3: A Teacher's Guide to Information Literacy for Grades K–2* by Annette C. H. Nelson and Danielle N. DuPuis. Santa Barbara, CA: Linworth. Copyright © 2010.

Name: _____Kindergarten

Snack Attack!

Problem: Kyra is hungry but can't have dinner until 6:30p.m.

Plan

Check off the box that shows your plan.

☐ Ask an adult for help   ☐ Call a friend

☐ Look in a cookbook   ☐ Look for a recipe on the Internet

Do

What should Kyra make?

_____

Draw pictures of the ingredients she will need on the back of this worksheet.

Review

Circle Yes or No to answer each question.

Did I do everything I was supposed to do?

Yes   No

Did I choose a recipe for Kyra to make and draw pictures of the ingredients?

Yes   No

From *The Adventures of Super3: A Teacher's Guide to Information Literacy for Grades K–2* by Annette C. H. Nelson and Danielle N. DuPuis. Santa Barbara, CA: Linworth. Copyright © 2010.

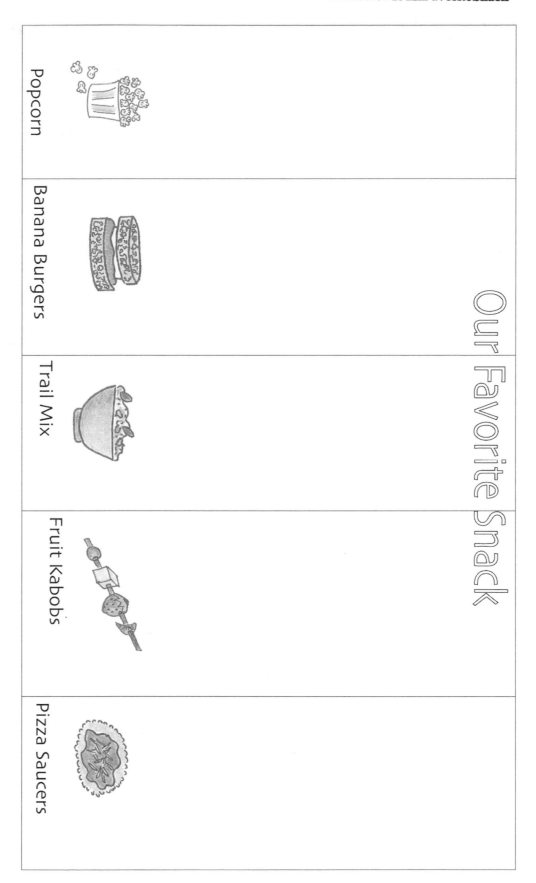

From *The Adventures of Super3: A Teacher's Guide to Information Literacy for Grades K–2* by Annette C. H. Nelson and Danielle N. DuPuis. Santa Barbara, CA: Linworth. Copyright © 2010.

Name: _____ 2nd Grade

Snack Attack!

Problem: Kyra is hungry but can't have dinner until 6:30p.m.

Plan

Write your plan in the spaces below.

I will help Kyra make a snack by _____

_____

Do

What should Kyra make?

_____

List the ingredients Kyra will need to make her snack.

_____

_____

Where did you find your recipe?

_____

Review

Circle Yes or No to answer each question.

Did I do everything I was supposed to do?

Yes   No

Did I choose a recipe for Kyra to make and list the ingredients she will need?

Yes   No

From *The Adventures of Super3: A Teacher's Guide to Information Literacy for Grades K–2* by Annette C. H. Nelson and Danielle N. DuPuis. Santa Barbara, CA: Linworth. Copyright © 2010.

CHAPTER 4

Second Grade Takes on Super3

Second graders provide teachers and teacher-librarians with an exciting opportunity to delve deeper into the information-seeking process. Students still love the blue-caped Super3 and enjoy applying the plan, do, and review strategies to the more complicated information literacy problems they often face. Though all these lessons are specifically designed for second grade, the provided modifications enable any kindergarten or first grade teacher to use them with his or her class. If an activity is too difficult or too easy for the ability level of your students, you can always use a modification provided.

The three lessons for this chapter gradually become more academic in nature. The first lesson begins with Maria losing her lunch on the way to school in "Super3 and the Lost Lunch." Second graders make a plan to help Maria retrace her morning to find the contents of her lunchbox. The second lesson, "Super3 and the Weather Worries," introduces Jenna and her concern about tomorrow's weather. Jenna plans to go with her father to the playground the following day but is not sure the weather will cooperate with her plans. Students can use various ways to determine the weather prediction for the following day. They can plan an outfit for Jenna to wear that prepares her for her playground trip. Here students face a familiar problem but are given the opportunity to solve it using unfamiliar methods (e.g., Internet search, weather hotline, newspaper article, etc.). Finally, in "Super3 and the Insect Investigation," Max faces a class assignment about insects. This lesson is designed to take two class periods of 40 minutes. Max's teacher assigns each student in his class an insect to research. Second graders determine that Max needs to research the life cycle of his insect (ladybug) and write a diary entry pretending to be a ladybug during one of its life stages. Once they create a plan to guide them through this process with Max, they can use various ways to determine the life cycle and then write the diary entry.

Lesson 1: Super3 and the Lost Lunch
Performance Objectives

+ Students will name the steps of the Super3.

+ Students will design a plan to help Maria find her lunch.

+ Students will examine a schedule to determine where Maria's lunch is located.

+ Students will implement their plan and review their work to determine its success.

Lesson Timeframe

30 minutes

Provided Materials

+ Copy of "Super3 and the Lost Lunch" comic (Gr2Less1Comic)—Display either a color transparency or electronic PDF version

+ Copy of "Super3 Step Cards" (Super3StepCards)

+ Lunchbox created from "Maria's Lunch" (Gr2Less1Lunch)

+ Copies for each student of "Super3 and the Lost Lunch" (Gr2Less1LostLunch)

+ Copy of "Plan Ideas" (Gr2Less1PlanIdeas)

+ Copy of "Maria's Schedule" (Gr2Less1Maria'sSchedule)—Display either a transparency or electronic PDF version

Materials You Will Need

+ Overhead projector or LCD projector and computer

+ Optional: Document camera

+ Pencils

+ Beach ball

Preparation Before Lesson

+ Create Maria's lunchbox and contents by following the directions included in "Maria's Lunch" (Gr2Less1Lunch).

+ For this lesson you will need to hide the contents of "Maria's Lunch" (Gr2Less1Lunch) in areas Maria visited before lunch. Options include: office, homeroom, gym, media center, classroom, or any of the hallways along the way to those places in your school.

Engagement

1. Have students sit in a circle. Roll the beach ball to a student. As you do so, name your favorite food to eat for lunch. Ask the student to do the same. Continue game play until all students in the class have the opportunity to name their favorite lunch food.

2. Display the "Super3 and the Lost Lunch" comic (Gr2Less1Comic).

3. Read the comic aloud and ask students what process Super3 should use to help him solve the problem (answer: the Super3).

4. Have students recall the steps of the Super3. Display each step as it is named by using the "Super3 Step Cards" (Super3StepCards).

Activity

5. Explain to the students that they need to solve the problem and will need to use the Super3 to find Maria's lost lunch.

6. Instruct students to think about what they could do to find the lunch that fell out of the lunchbox. Give them time to think and then share as a class. As students come up with ideas write each one on the board or display the "Plan Ideas" (Gr2Less1PlanIdeas).

7. Discuss the different options for finding the lunch and discuss positives and negatives for each possible plan.

   - Ask a friend. But are there any friends around? And a friend might not know where the lunch is located.

   - Ask a teacher. But are teachers eating lunch already? Are teachers too busy to help look for the lost lunch?

   - Check the lost and found. Usually it's just for jackets and lunchboxes, not food.

   - Retrace her steps. This is the best option to find out where the lunch is—you'll be able to search each place and see if there is anything there.

8. After the class decides that retracing Maria's steps is the best idea, ask them what information they would need to know in order to do that (e.g., where she was before lunch).

9. Distribute copies of "Super3 and the Lost Lunch" (Gr2Less1LostLunch) to each student.

10. Display a copy of "Super3 and the Lost Lunch" (Gr2Less1LostLunch) and assist students in reading the directions.

11. Display a copy of "Maria's Schedule" (Gr2Less1Maria'sSchedule) and allow students time to discuss places they could look to find her lunch based on her morning activities.

12. Have students list the places they will look for Maria's lunch on their paper as you list them on the projected copy.

13. Ask students which step of the Super3 comes next (Do). Explain to students that as a class they will follow their plan (retrace Maria's steps) and find the lunch. As a group, go to the places in order and allow students time to look around and find the previously

hidden elements of Maria's lunch. When students find a piece of her lunch they can place it inside the file-folder lunchbox.

14. Once all the pieces of lunch are discovered, return to the Media Center and review the process and product (locating Maria's lunch).

15. Have students answer the review questions on their worksheet, "Super3 and the Lost Lunch" (Gr2Less1LostLunch).

Closure

16. Gather students back together and ask them to recall the three steps of the Super3 and explain how they used the steps to solve Maria's problem of locating her lost lunch.

Assessment

17. Collect and grade the worksheet, "Super3 and the Lost Lunch" (Gr2Less1LostLunch).

Modifications

For Use with Kindergarten

✦ Present the problem as Maria having lost her *lunchbox* instead of the contents of her lunch. When creating the plan with the students, guide students to plan to look in the lost and found for her lunchbox.

✦ Use the kindergarten modified version of "Super3 and the Lost Lunch" (Gr2Less1ModKLostLunch).

For Use with First Grade

✦ Present the problem as Maria having lost the contents of her lunch as you would for second grade. However, use the first grade modified version of "Super3 and the Lost Lunch" (Gr2Less1Mod1LostLunch).

Suggested Books

Barrett, Judi. *Cloudy with a Chance of Meatballs.* New York: Aladdin, 1982.

Fleming, Denise. *Lunch.* New York: Henry Holt and Co., 1992.

Harris, Lee. *Never Let Your Cat Make Lunch for You.* Berkeley, CA: Tricycle Press, 1999.

Thaler, Mike. *The Cafeteria Lady from the Black Lagoon.* New York: Scholastic, 1998.

Viorst, Judith. *Alexander and the Terrible, Horrible, No Good, Very Bad Day.* New York: Aladdin, 1987.

Wells, Rosemary. *Yoko.* New York: Hyperion Books for Children, 1998.

Maria's Lunch

What you'll need to create Maria's lunch

- ✦ 2 pieces of 8 ½ x 11 cardstock
- ✦ Color printer
- ✦ 4 Velcro dots
- ✦ 1 manila file folder
- ✦ Access to a laminator
- ✦ Exacto knife

Preparation:

1. Print out the attached pieces onto cardstock using a color printer.
2. Cut out the pieces.
3. Glue the "lunchbox" piece onto a folded file folder.
4. Cut around the edges of the folder (with the exception of the bottom—you want the folder to be able to fold) and cut out the inside of the handle (you may need to use an exacto knife).
5. Laminate all of the pieces as well as the file folder.
6. Cut out the pieces.
7. Using sticky Velcro pieces, attach the food pieces inside the lunchbox.

Directions for Use:

1. Using the schedule, "Maria's Day," scatter the food pieces in the various places that Maria visited throughout the day before lunch. After students have created a plan for finding the lunch pieces, "do" the activity of finding the pieces by going on a scavenger hunt around the school. You may wish to tape these pieces to the walls or floor to make them stand out.

From *The Adventures of Super3: A Teacher's Guide to Information Literacy for Grades K–2* by Annette C. H. Nelson and Danielle N. DuPuis. Santa Barbara, CA: Linworth. Copyright © 2010.

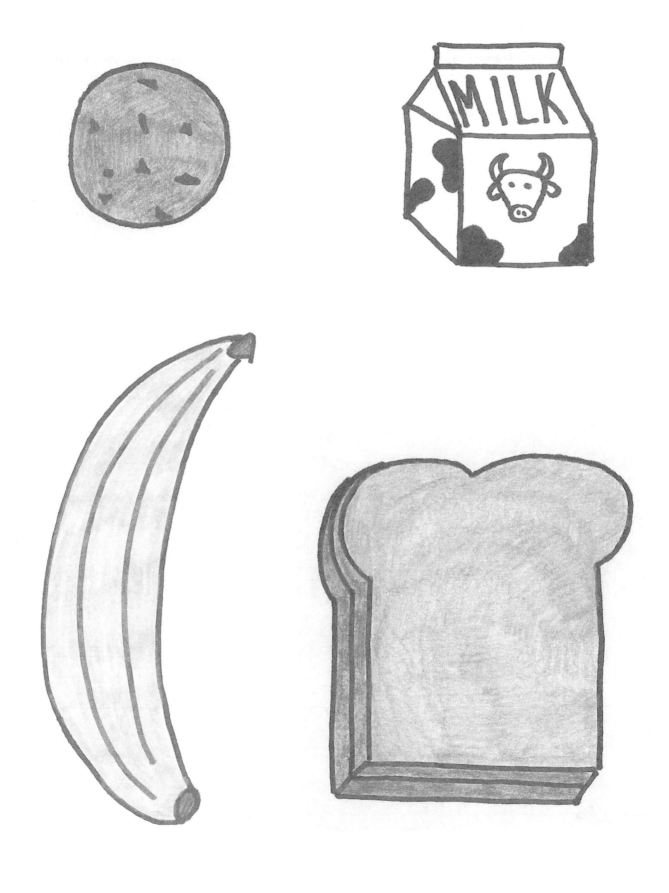

From *The Adventures of Super3: A Teacher's Guide to Information Literacy for Grades K–2* by Annette C. H. Nelson and Danielle N. DuPuis. Santa Barbara, CA: Linworth. Copyright © 2010.

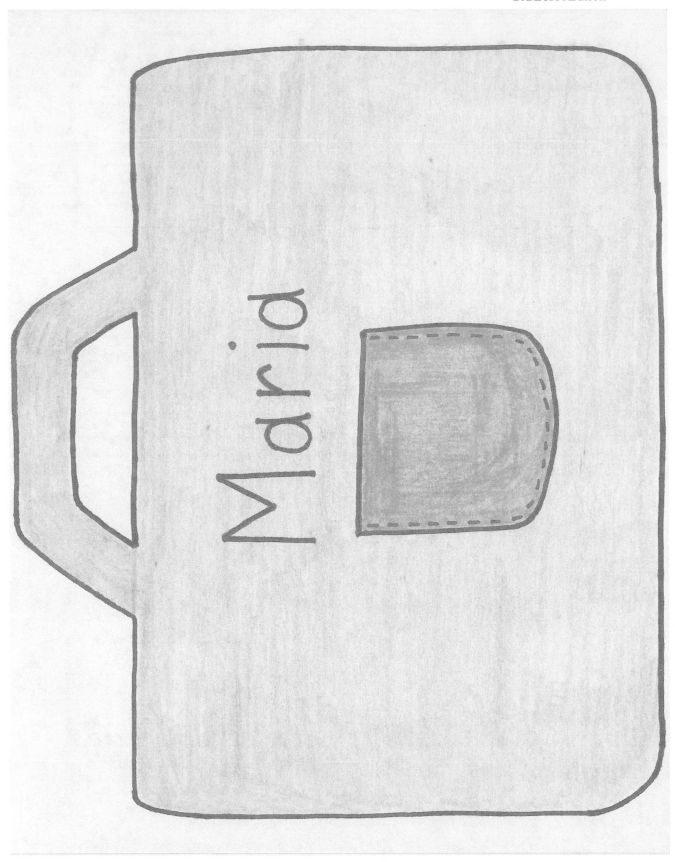

From *The Adventures of Super3: A Teacher's Guide to Information Literacy for Grades K–2* by Annette C. H. Nelson 100 and Danielle N. DuPuis. Santa Barbara, CA: Linworth. Copyright © 2010.

Name: _____ 2nd grade

Super3 and the Lost Lunch

Problem: Maria's lunch fell out of her lunch box. She had 4 things for lunch.

Plan

First, retrace Maria's steps. Next, list all of the places you will look for her lunch.

_____

_____

Do

Okay, now let's go look to see if we can find Maria's lost lunch!

Review

Circle Yes or No to answer each question.

Did I find all four pieces of Maria's lunch?

Yes   No

Could I use the Super3 the next time I have something that is lost?

Yes   No

Is there anything I need to do before I give Maria her lunchbox?

Yes   No

From *The Adventures of Super3: A Teacher's Guide to Information Literacy for Grades K–2* by Annette C. H. Nelson and Danielle N. DuPuis. Santa Barbara, CA: Linworth. Copyright © 2010.

Plan Ideas

Directions: Print out the attached cue cards onto cardstock, laminate, and cut out. If you have a magnetic board in your classroom/library, adding a magnetic strip to the back will allow for easy manipulation of the pieces on the board.

Retrace your steps

Ask a Friend

Ask a teacher

Lost and Found

From *The Adventures of Super3: A Teacher's Guide to Information Literacy for Grades K–2* by Annette C. H. Nelson 102 and Danielle N. DuPuis. Santa Barbara, CA: Linworth. Copyright © 2010.

Maria's Schedule

9:00a.m.	Checked in at the Office for being late to school
9:10a.m.	Homeroom
9:25a.m.	Math Class
10:40a.m.	P.E. Class in the Gym
11:10a.m.	Media Class
11:40 a.m.	Lunch
12:10p.m.	Recess on the Playground
12:40p.m.	Reading Class
2:00p.m.	Science Class
2:40p.m.	Technology Class in the Computer Lab

From *The Adventures of Super3: A Teacher's Guide to Information Literacy for Grades K–2* by Annette C. H. Nelson and Danielle N. DuPuis. Santa Barbara, CA: Linworth. Copyright © 2010.

Name: _____Kindergarten

Super3 and the Lost Lunch

Problem: Maria has lost her lunch box!

Plan

Use a crayon to draw a box around the best plan to help Maria find her lunch box.

1. Retrace Maria's steps

2. Ask a friend for help

3. Ask a teacher for help

4. Look in the lost and found

Do

Okay, now let's go look to see if we can find Maria's lost lunch box!

Review

Circle Yes or No to answer each question.

Did I find Maria's lunch box?

Yes   No

Could I use the Super3 the next time I have something that is lost?

Yes   No

Is there anything I need to do before I give Maria her lunchbox?

Yes   No

From *The Adventures of Super3: A Teacher's Guide to Information Literacy for Grades K–2* by Annette C. H. Nelson and Danielle N. DuPuis. Santa Barbara, CA: Linworth. Copyright © 2010.

Name: _____ 1st grade

Super3 and the Lost Lunch

Problem: Maria's lunch fell out of her lunch box.

Plan

First, retrace your steps. Next, circle all of the places you will look.

Lunchroom	Math Class	Office	Media Center
Gym	Homeroom	Music	Art
Computer room	Lunchroom	Bus	Science Class

Do

Okay, now let's go look to see if we can find Maria's lost lunch!

Review

Circle Yes or No to answer each question.

Did I find all four pieces of Maria's lunch?

Yes   No

Could I use the Super3 the next time I have something that is lost?

Yes   No

Is there anything I need to do before I give Maria her lunchbox?

Yes   No

From *The Adventures of Super3: A Teacher's Guide to Information Literacy for Grades K–2* by Annette C. H. Nelson and Danielle N. DuPuis. Santa Barbara, CA: Linworth. Copyright © 2010.

Lesson 2: Super3 and the Weather Worries
Performance Objectives

✦ Students will design a plan to determine the following day's weather.

✦ Students will create an outfit for Jenna to wear based on the weather forecast.

Lesson Timeframe

35 minutes

Provided Materials

✦ Copy of "Super3 and the Weather Worries" comic (Gr2Less2Comic)—Display either a color transparency or electronic PDF version

✦ Copies for each student of "Weather Worries" (Gr2Less2WeatherWorries)

✦ Copies for each student of "What To Wear" (Gr2Less2WhatToWear)

✦ Copy of "Super3 Step Cards" (Super3StepCards)

Materials You Will Need

✦ Overhead projector or LCD projector and computer

✦ Optional: Document camera

✦ Pencils

Preparation Before Lesson

✦ Read over the lesson and determine which idea for the plan you would like the students to use to solve the problem.

✦ Gather the materials needed to complete your selected plan (e.g., newspapers, telephone with speakerphone, or computers with Internet access).

Engagement

1. Display "Super3 and the Weather Worries" comic (Gr2Less2Comic).

2. Read the comic aloud and ask students what process Jenna should use to help solve her problem (answer: the Super3).

3. Have students recall the steps of the Super3 and display each step as they name it using the "Super3 Step Cards" (Super3Stepcards).

Activity

4. Explain to students that they need to solve Jenna's problem by using the Super3 to find out the weather for the following day.

5. Distribute copies of "Weather Worries" (Gr2Less2WeatherWorries) to each student.

6. Project a transparency or electronic copy of the worksheet and assist students in reading the directions.

7. Instruct students to think about what they could do to find out the weather for the following day in your area. Give students time to think of a plan on their own, then time to discuss with the people sitting near them, and finally, time to share their ideas with the class.

8. As students come up with ideas, write each one on the board. Possible suggestions include:

   - Check a Web site such as The Weather Channel, http://www.weather.com/.
   - Read a newspaper
   - Watch the news
   - Call a weather hotline—(Your Area Code) 936-1212
   - Ask a friend
   - Go outside to look

9. After students brainstorm, discuss the different options for determining the weather and discuss positives and negatives for each possible plan.

   - Ask a friend.Do you have any friends around that you could ask? Is a friend a reliable source for this type of information?
   - Check a Web site. Do you have Internet access?
   - Read a newspaper. Is it easy to find the weather report in the newspaper? Do you have a newspaper around?
   - Call a weather hotline. Do you have access to a phone?
   - Go outside to look. Will this tell you the weather for tomorrow?

10. Choose a plan as a class and have students record it on their worksheet.

11. Move on to the "Do" step and have students carry out their selected plan.

12. Instruct students to record the temperature and a description of the weather for the next day. (cloudy, sunny, rainy, foggy, snowy, etc.)

13. Then have students review their process and product.

14. Collect the "Weather Worries" (Gr2Less2WeatherWorries) and present the students with a new problem.

15. Explain that Jenna doesn't know what to wear for her day at the park. Tell the students they need to dress Jenna based on the weather forecast they just discovered.

16. Distribute copies of "What To Wear" (Gr2Less2WhatToWear) and have students draw on the appropriate clothing for Jenna's park adventure.

Closure

17. Ask students to recall the steps of the Super3 and explain how they used the steps to solve Jenna's weather worries.

Assessment

18. Collect and grade "Weather Worries" (Gr2Less2WeatherWorries) and "What to Wear" (Gr2Less2WhatToWear).

Modifications

For Use with Kindergarten

✦ Visit The Weather Channel, http://www.weather.com/ using a computer and LCD projector as a class, or use a telephone with speakerphone to call the weather hotline in your area.

✦ Use the kindergarten modified versions of "Weather Worries" (Gr2Less2ModKWeather-Worries) and "What to Wear" (Gr2Less2ModKWhatToWear).

For Use with First Grade

✦ Visit The Weather Channel, http://www.weather.com/ using a computer and LCD projector as a class, or use a telephone with speakerphone to call the weather hotline in your area.

✦ Use the first grade modified versions of "Weather Worries" (Gr2Less2Mod1Weather Worries) and "What to Wear" (Gr2Less2Mod1WhatToWear).

Suggested Books

Barrett, Judi. *Cloudy with a Chance of Meatballs.* New York: Aladdin Books, 1982.

Bauer, Marion Dane. *If Frogs Made the Weather.* New York: Holiday House, 2005.

Franson, Scott E. *Un-brella.* New Milford, CT: Roaring Brook Press, 2007.

Hesse, Karen. *Come On, Rain.* New York: Scholastic, 1999.

Schmidt, Karen Lee. *Carl's Nose.* Orlando, FL: Harcourt, 2006.

Name: _____2nd Grade

Weather Worries

Problem: Jenna needs to know tomorrow's weather.

Plan

Write your plan in the space provided.

I will _____

_____

_____

Do

Tomorrow, the temperature will be _____ degrees Fahrenheit.

Describe the weather for tomorrow._____

_____

_____

Review

Circle or write your answer to the questions.

Did I do everything I was supposed to do?

Yes   No

What clothes should Jenna wear tomorrow?

_____

From *The Adventures of Super3: A Teacher's Guide to Information Literacy for Grades K–2* by Annette C. H. Nelson and Danielle N. DuPuis. Santa Barbara, CA: Linworth. Copyright © 2010.

Name: _____ 2nd Grade

What to Wear

What will Jenna wear for her outing in the park tomorrow? Draw the appropriate clothes on Jenna for her outing tomorrow. Color your finished picture.

From *The Adventures of Super3: A Teacher's Guide to Information Literacy for Grades K–2* by Annette C. H. Nelson and Danielle N. DuPuis. Santa Barbara, CA: Linworth. Copyright © 2010.

Name: _____ Kindergarten

Weather Worries

Problem: Jenna needs to know tomorrow's weather.

Plan

Check off the box that shows your plan.

☐ Watch the news.   ☐ Ask a friend.

☐ Go to www.weather.com   ☐ Go outside and look.

☐ Call weather hotline.   ☐ Read the newspaper.

Do

The temperature will be _____ degrees Fahrenheit

What does the weather look like for tomorrow? Circle your answer.

Sunny	Snowy	Cloudy
Windy	Rainy	Foggy

Review

Circle or write your answer to the questions.

Did I do everything I was supposed to do?

Yes   No

What clothes should Jenna wear tomorrow?

_____

From *The Adventures of Super3: A Teacher's Guide to Information Literacy for Grades K–2* by Annette C. H. Nelson and Danielle N. DuPuis. Santa Barbara, CA: Linworth. Copyright © 2010.

Name: _____ Kindergarten

What to Wear

What will Jenna wear for her outing in the park tomorrow? Color the clothes she will need and place an X through the clothes she will not need.

From *The Adventures of Super3: A Teacher's Guide to Information Literacy for Grades K–2* by Annette C. H. Nelson and Danielle N. DuPuis. Santa Barbara, CA: Linworth. Copyright © 2010.

113

Name: _____1st Grade

Weather Worries

Problem: Jenna needs to know tomorrow's weather.

Plan   Check off the box that shows your plan.

☐ Watch the news.

☐ Go to www.weather.com

☐ Call weather hotline.

☐ Ask a friend.

☐ Go outside and look.

☐ Read the newspaper.

Do

The temperature will be _____ degrees Fahrenheit

Describe the weather for tomorrow. _____

_____

_____

Review   Did I do everything I was supposed to do?

Yes   No

| Circle or write your answer to the questions. |

What clothes should Jenna wear tomorrow?

_____

From *The Adventures of Super3: A Teacher's Guide to Information Literacy for Grades K–2* by Annette C. H. Nelson and Danielle N. DuPuis. Santa Barbara, CA: Linworth. Copyright © 2010.

What to Wear? Name: _____

1st Grade

What will Jenna wear for her outing in the park tomorrow? Select and color the proper clothes she will need. Cut out Jenna and the clothing she will need to make your own paper doll.

From *The Adventures of Super3: A Teacher's Guide to Information Literacy for Grades K–2* by Annette C. H. Nelson and Danielle N. DuPuis. Santa Barbara, CA: Linworth. Copyright © 2010.

Lesson 3: Super3 and the Insect Investigation
Performance Objectives

- ✦ Students will recall the steps of the Super3.
- ✦ Students will create a poster showing the life cycle of a ladybug.
- ✦ Students will compose a diary entry describing a stage of a ladybug's life.
- ✦ Students will evaluate their product and information-seeking process.

Lesson Timeframe

60 minutes (one class period, or two 30-minute sessions)

Provided Materials

- ✦ Copy of "Super3 and the Insect Investigation" comic (Gr2Less3Comic)—Display either a color transparency or electronic PDF version
- ✦ Copy of "Insect Investigation" (Gr2Less3InsectInvestigation)—Display either as a transparency or using an LCD projector and computer
- ✦ Copies for each student of "A Ladybug's Life" (Gr2Less3LadybugLife)
- ✦ Copy of "Poster Rubric" (Gr2Less3PosterRubric)—Display either as a transparency or using an LCD projector and computer
- ✦ Copy of "Plan" (Gr2Less3Plan)—Display either as a transparency or using an LCD projector and computer
- ✦ Copy of "Super3 Step Cards" (Super3StepCards)
- ✦ Copies for each student of "Review" (Gr2Less3Review)
- ✦ Copies for each student of "Dear Diary" (Gr2Less3Diary)

Materials You Will Need

- ✦ Overhead projector or LCD projector and computer
- ✦ Optional: Document camera
- ✦ Pencils

Preparation Before Lesson

- ✦ Read over the lesson and determine *where* you would like students to find their information for the life cycle of a ladybug.

✦ Gather the materials necessary for the students to research. (e.g., computers with Internet access and links to Web sites, encyclopedias, nonfiction books about ladybugs, magazine articles, or information printed from the Internet).

Engagement

1. Display "Super3 and the Insect Investigation" comic (Gr2Less3Comic).

2. Read the comic aloud and ask students what process Max should use to help solve his problem (answer: the Super3).

3. Have students recall the steps of the Super3. Display each step as it is named using the "Super3 Step Cards" (Super3StepCards).

Activity

4. Explain to the students that they need to help Max complete his assignment. The students will need to understand his assignment before they can help him.

5. Display a copy of "Insect Investigation" (Gr2Less3InsectInvestigation) and read the assignment together.

6. Display a copy of "Poster Rubric" (Gr2Less3PosterRubric) and read over what the students need to do for their assignment.

7. Discuss what Max needs to do in order to complete his assignment (research the life cycle of a ladybug / draw the different stages / write a diary entry pretending to be a ladybug in the life cycle stage of their choice).

8. Display a copy of "Plan" (Gr2Less3Plan) and write the plan that the class decides to do.

9. Discuss the different options for researching the stages of ladybug life and discuss positives and negatives for each possible plan.

   • Selected Web sites on the Internet

   • Nonfiction books about ladybugs

   • Magazine articles about ladybugs

   • Encyclopedia article on ladybugs

10. Record the student ideas for research on the plan sheet and circle the one the class chooses to do.

11. Distribute copies of "A Ladybug's Life" (Gr2Less3LadybugLife) and allow students time to research and illustrate the life cycles of the ladybug.

12. Have students decide the stage of the ladybug's life they wish to portray and complete their diary entry on "Dear Diary" (Gr2Less3Diary).

13. Circulate and assist students throughout the research and diary entry creation.

14. Once students complete their diary entry, have some volunteers from the class share their entry with the class. See if the class can determine which part of the life cycle the student chose by their diary entry.

15. Distribute copies of the "Review" (Gr2Less3Review). Display a copy of the "Review" sheet and assist students in evaluating their product and information-seeking process.

Closure

16. Gather students back together and ask them to recall the steps of the Super3 and explain how they used the steps to help Max complete his research project.

Assessment

17. Collect and grade "A Ladybug's Life" (Gr2Less3LadybugLife), "Dear Diary" (Gr2-Less3Diary), and "Review" (Gr2Less3Review).

Modifications

For Use with Kindergarten

✦ When presenting the problem, use the kindergarten / first grade modified version of the resource sheets, "Insect Investigation" (Gr2Less3ModK&1InsectInvestigation) and "Poster Rubric" (Gr2Less3ModK&1PosterRubric). In these versions, students will only determine the life cycle stages of the ladybug and draw them.

✦ Model how to research the life cycle as a class by using a computer with Internet access and an LCD projector, or by reading a nonfiction book about ladybugs.

✦ Use the kindergarten modified version of "A Ladybug's Life" (Gr2Less3ModKLadybug-Life). This version includes pictures of the life cycle that students can cut out and glue on instead of drawing if you wish. The pictures are on a half-sheet.

✦ For reviewing the project, use the kindergarten/ first grade modified "Review" (Gr2Less3ModK&1Review). This can be copied on the back of the "Insect Investigation" sheet.

For Use with First Grade

✦ When presenting the problem, use the kindergarten/ first grade modified version of the resource sheets, "Insect Investigation" (Gr2Less3ModK&1InsectInvestigation) and "Poster Rubric" (Gr2Less3ModK&1PosterRubric). In these versions, students will only determine the life cycle stages of the ladybug and draw them.

✦ Research a ladybug's life cycle in a way that is appropriate to the level of your students by modeling to the class or allowing students to independently research.

✦ Use the first grade modified version of "A Ladybug's Life" (Gr2Less3Mod1Ladybug-Life). If you feel your class needs more assistance, you can use the half-sheet of pictures from the kindergarten modified version of the worksheet, "A Ladybug's Life" (Gr2Less3ModKLadybugLife).

✦ For reviewing the project, use the kindergarten/ first grade modified "Review" (Gr2Less-3ModK&1Review). This can be copied on the back of the "Insect Investigation" sheet.

Suggested Books

Carle, Eric. *The Grouchy Ladybug.* 1977. New York: Harper Collins, 1996.

Cronin, Doreen. *Diary of a Fly.* New York: Harper Collins, 2007.

Laden, Nina. *Roberto, the Insect Architect.* San Francisco: Chronicle Books, 2000.

Marsico, Katie. *A Ladybug Larva Grows Up.* New York: Children's Press, 2007.

O'Connor, Jane. *Fancy Nancy: Bonjour, Butterfly.* New York: Harper Collins, 2008.

O'Malley, Kevin. *Leo Cockroach: Toy Tester.* New York: Walker Books, 2001

Rockwell, Anne. *Bugs Are Insects.* New York: Harper Collins, 2001.

120

Insect Investigation

Dear Families,

   Your child has been learning about insects in science class. For their monthly project, they have been assigned an insect to research. Your child needs to complete the attached poster on the life cycle of the insect they have been assigned. After completing the poster, they should select a stage from the insect's life cycle to write about. Then, they should write a diary entry telling about their day from their insect's point of view. Please feel free to contact me if you have any questions or concerns.

Sincerely,

Ms. Barkly

From *The Adventures of Super3: A Teacher's Guide to Information Literacy for Grades K–2* by Annette C. H. Nelson and Danielle N. DuPuis. Santa Barbara, CA: Linworth. Copyright © 2010.

Name:_____2nd grade

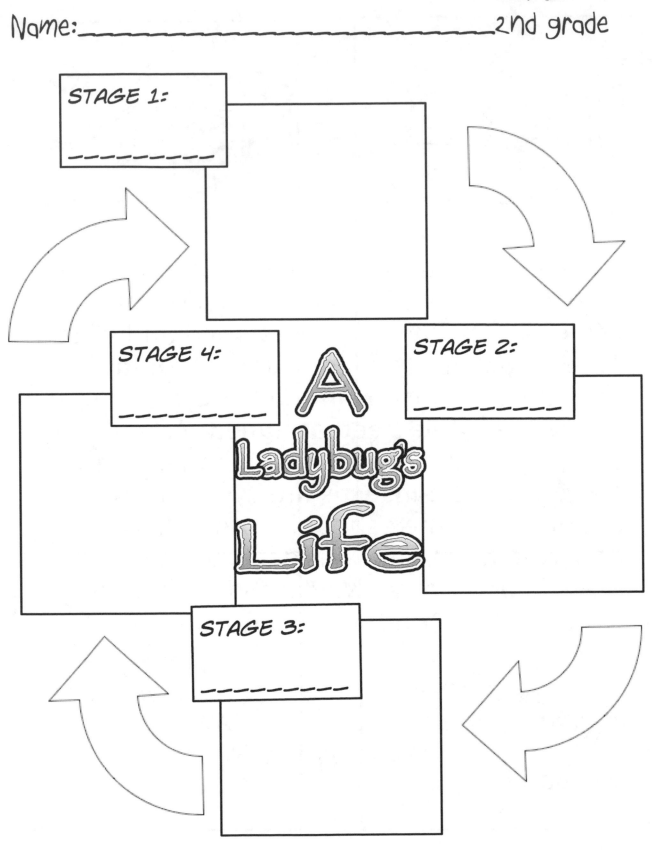

STAGE 1:

_ _ _ _ _ _ _ _ _

STAGE 4:

_ _ _ _ _ _ _ _ _

A Ladybug's Life

STAGE 2:

_ _ _ _ _ _ _ _ _

STAGE 3:

_ _ _ _ _ _ _ _ _

 From *The Adventures of Super3: A Teacher's Guide to Information Literacy for Grades K–2* by Annette C. H. Nelson and Danielle N. DuPuis. Santa Barbara, CA: Linworth. Copyright © 2010.

Here are the requirements for the Insect Investigation. I will use this to grade your project. Make sure to look this over so you know what is expected of you.

--Ms. Barkly

What you need to do	Possible Points	Points Earned
Draw the four stages of your insect's life	10	
Label your drawing correctly	5	
Write a diary entry pretending to be your insect in the stage of life of your choice.	10	
Use correct diary format	5	
Check your work for capitalization, usage, punctuation, and spelling. (CUPS)	10	
Total	40	

From *The Adventures of Super3: A Teacher's Guide to Information Literacy for Grades K–2* by Annette C. H. Nelson and Danielle N. DuPuis. Santa Barbara, CA: Linworth. Copyright © 2010.

Plan

What does Max need to do for his Insect Investigation?

Insect assigned: _____

Research needed: _____

Complete: _____

Pick a: _____

Write a: _____

Where should we help Max get his information?

• _____

• _____

• _____

Now circle the best source.

From *The Adventures of Super3: A Teacher's Guide to Information Literacy for Grades K–2* by Annette C. H. Nelson and Danielle N. DuPuis. Santa Barbara, CA: Linworth. Copyright © 2010.

Name: _____2nd Grade

Review your Product:

1. Did you draw the life cycle of your ladybug and fill in the labels? _____

2. Did you write a diary entry pretending you were a ladybug? _____

3. Did you put your name on all your papers? _____

4. Did you make sure to check for correct spelling and grammar? _____

5. Are you proud of your work? _____

Review Your Process:

1. What did you do well this time? _____

_____

2. Where did you find your information?_____

_____

3. Was it a good place to look?

_____

From *The Adventures of Super3: A Teacher's Guide to Information Literacy for Grades K–2* by Annette C. H. Nelson and Danielle N. DuPuis. Santa Barbara, CA: Linworth. Copyright © 2010.

Today's Date _____

Dear Diary,

It's great being in the_____ stage of life.

Today I _____

_____

_____

Tomorrow I hope to _____

_____

_____

I love being a ladybug!

Sincerely,

_____

From *The Adventures of Super3: A Teacher's Guide to Information Literacy for Grades K–2* by Annette C. H. Nelson
126 and Danielle N. DuPuis. Santa Barbara, CA: Linworth. Copyright © 2010.

Insect Investigation

Dear Students,

   You have learned about insects in science class. I would like for you to learn more about the insect, the ladybug. Find out what the life cycle of the ladybug looks like. Then complete the poster to show what you learned.

Sincerely,

Ms. Barkly

From *The Adventures of Super3: A Teacher's Guide to Information Literacy for Grades K–2* by Annette C. H. Nelson and Danielle N. DuPuis. Santa Barbara, CA: Linworth. Copyright © 2010.

Here are the requirements for the Insect Investigation. I will use this to grade your project. Make sure to look this over so you know what is expected of you.

--Ms. Barkly

What you need to do	Possible Points	Points Earned
Draw the four stages of your insect's life	10	
Label your drawing correctly	5	
Check your work for capitalization, usage, punctuation, and spelling. (CUPS)	10	
Total	25	

From *The Adventures of Super3: A Teacher's Guide to Information Literacy for Grades K–2* by Annette C. H. Nelson and Danielle N. DuPuis. Santa Barbara, CA: Linworth. Copyright © 2010.

Name:_____Kindergarten

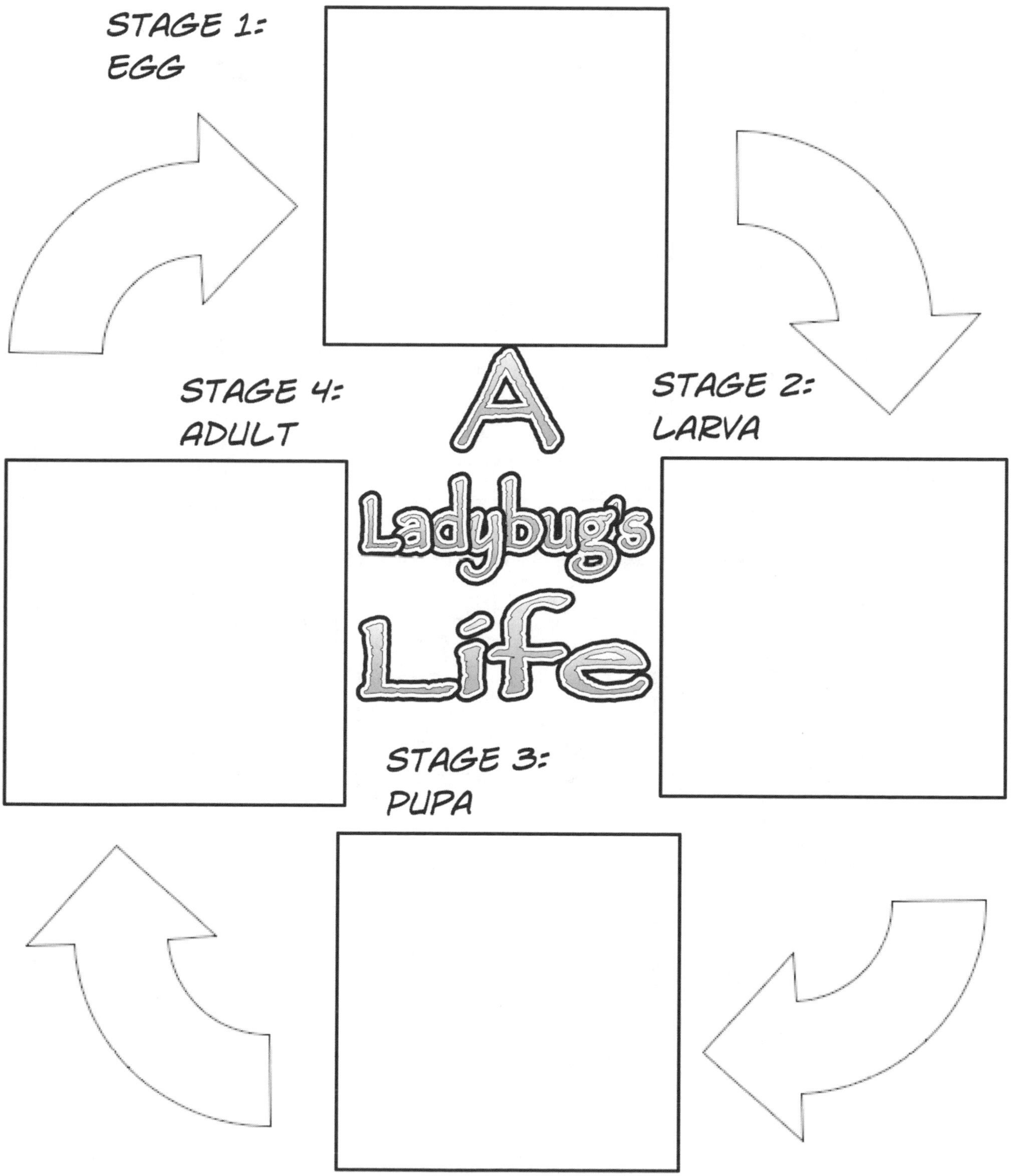

STAGE 1:
EGG

STAGE 4:
ADULT

A
Ladybug's
Life

STAGE 2:
LARVA

STAGE 3:
PUPA

From *The Adventures of Super3: A Teacher's Guide to Information Literacy for Grades K–2* by Annette C. H. Nelson and Danielle N. DuPuis. Santa Barbara, CA: Linworth. Copyright © 2010.

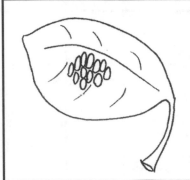

DIRECTIONS:

CUT OUT EACH SQUARE. GLUE INTO THE CORRECT SPACE ON YOUR LADYBUG'S LIFE POSTER.

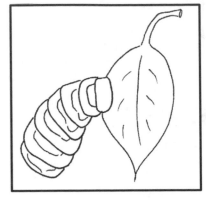

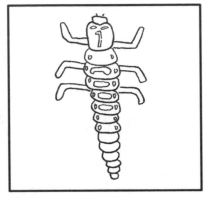

DIRECTIONS:

CUT OUT EACH SQUARE. GLUE INTO THE CORRECT SPACE ON YOUR LADYBUG'S LIFE POSTER.

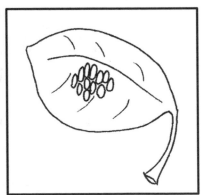

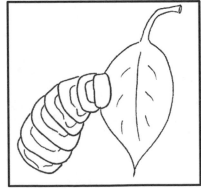

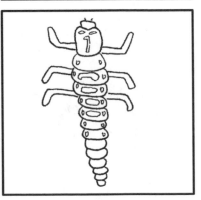

From *The Adventures of Super3: A Teacher's Guide to Information Literacy for Grades K–2* by Annette C. H. Nelson and Danielle N. DuPuis. Santa Barbara, CA: Linworth. Copyright © 2010.

Name: _____

Review

Circle your answer.

Review your Product:

1. Did you complete your ladybug life cycle poster?

Yes   No

2. Did you put your name on all your papers?

Yes   No

3. Are you proud of your work?

Yes   No

Review Your Process:

1. Where did you find your information?

Web site   Nonfiction book   Magazine

2. Was it a good place to look? _____

_____

From *The Adventures of Super3: A Teacher's Guide to Information Literacy for Grades K–2* by Annette C. H. Nelson and Danielle N. DuPuis. Santa Barbara, CA: Linworth. Copyright © 2010.

Name:_____1st grade

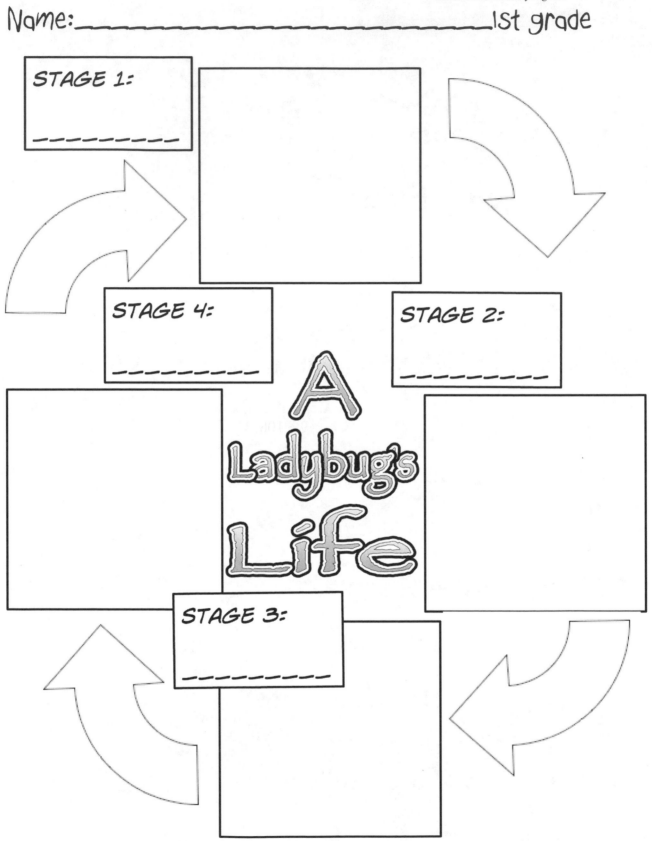

STAGE 1:

_____

STAGE 4:

_____

STAGE 2:

_____

A Ladybug's Life

STAGE 3:

_____

From *The Adventures of Super3: A Teacher's Guide to Information Literacy for Grades K–2* by Annette C. H. Nelson
132 and Danielle N. DuPuis. Santa Barbara, CA: Linworth. Copyright © 2010.

Index